Ira Moskowit '74

A Little Boy in Search of God

Mysticism in a Personal Light

By Isaac Bashevis Singer

THE FAMILY MOSKAT

SATAN IN GORAY

GIMPEL THE FOOL

THE SPINOZA OF MARKET STREET

THE MAGICIAN OF LUBLIN

THE SLAVE

SHORT FRIDAY AND OTHER STORIES

THE MANOR

THE ESTATE

THE SEANCE

A FRIEND OF KAFKA

A CROWN OF FEATHERS

IN MY FATHER'S COURT

ENEMIES, A LOVE STORY

PASSIONS

By Isaac Bashevis Singer and Ira Moskowitz

THE HASIDIM

By Ira Moskowitz

AMERICAN INDIAN CEREMONIAL DANCES

GREAT DRAWINGS OF ALL TIME

A Little Boy in Search of God

Mysticism in a Personal Light

Isaac Bashevis Singer
and Ira Moskowitz

1976

Doubleday & Company, Inc., Garden City, New York

Chapter 10 first appeared in *Midstream: A Monthly Jewish Review.*

Library of Congress Cataloging in Publication Data

Singer, Isaac Bashevis, 1904–
A little boy in search of God.

1. Singer, Isaac Bashevis, 1904– —Biography—
Youth. 2. Singer, Isaac Bashevis, 1904– —Religion
and ethics. I. Moskowitz, Ira, joint author.
II. Title.
PJ5129.S49Z524   839'.09'33 [B]
ISBN 0-385-06653-8
Library of Congress Catalog Card Number 75–6078

Mysticism isn't a line of thought separated from religion. They both share a basis in the human soul—the feeling that the world is no accident or blind force and that the human spirit and body are closely linked with the universe and its Creator. The pagan who made a god of stone knew full well that this stone by itself could neither hear nor help him. He often carved it himself, but this stone was part of the rocks, the mountains, the rivers—of all nature. When addressing this stone, the idolator spoke to Creation and to its forces. Primitive as he might have been, he felt somewhere within him that if one learned the essence of this stone, its origin and its secret, one would know everything. The idol to him was the symbol of the mystery of the world. Those who deified animals or men had similar feelings.

If there is a difference between religion and mysticism, it consists of the fact that religion is almost completely dependent upon revelation. All religions have preached that God revealed Himself to a prophet and communicated His demands through him. Religion never remained the property of a single individual. It appealed to a group. It often tended to proliferate and take in whole tribes and nations. Religious leaders often forced obeisance to their faith with the sword. Because of this, religion tended in time to become routine and closely linked with social systems. Mysticism, on the other hand, is individualistic. True mysticism has always belonged to one person or to a small group. It was and it has remained esoteric. The mystic never completely relied upon the revelations of others but sought God in his own fashion. The mystic often assumed the religion of his environment, but he tried to extend it by coupling it with the higher powers; actually, to become a prophet himself.

My personal definition of religion is a mysticism that has been transformed into a discipline, a mass experience, and thus grown partially diluted and often worldly. The more successful a religion is, the stronger its influence, the further it recedes from its mystical origin. Dogma and magic take the place of spiritual experience. Since the basis of every religion is mysticism, and later other elements come to dominate it, every religion is full of contradictions, and these contradictions grow in ratio with its popularity and the number of its adherents. Since the mystic is by nature an individualist and frequently a person who feels responsible only for himself, he can be more or less complete and honest. The moment the mystic acquires disciples and followers his mysticism begins to share the fate of religion. Differences of opinion crop up along with silent and open conflicts, and the obstacles and temptations of worldliness begin to obtrude.

In essence, every mystic is a doubter. He is by nature a seeker. Mysticism and skepticism are not contradictory. The mystic gropes in the dark. He waits for revelation, but either it doesn't come or it comes seldom. Often he grows despondent in this search. But mysticism isn't simply skepticism or agnosticism. Sooner or later the mystic tends to convince himself or to fall under the illusion that he has discovered something. Mystics are by nature enthusiasts. The fire of faith that burns within them cannot coexist for long with the ice of skepticism. When the mystic begins to sense that he has discovered some truth, he fits it within the framework of his religion. Jewish mystics related their discoveries to passages in the Scriptures, the Gemara, the Midrash, even to Jewish customs. Christian mystics based their findings on the New Testament. But since the character of the mystic is alike in Jew, Christian, and Moslem, a kinship exists among all mystics. There is a greater similarity between Swedenborg and Haim Vital or Rabbi Nachman Braclawer than, let us say, between the Vilna Gaon and the pope of his time.

There is a similarity not only between the explorations of the mystics but between their findings as well. The mystic realizes that God is silent in word and tongue, but that He speaks in deeds. Every mystic believes in Divine Providence. God's deeds and the fashion in which He guides the destiny of man and the world constitute His speech. There is no dictionary for this language, nor can there be. Such a dictionary would possibly be the size of the universe. God speaks simultaneously in a person's brain, in the center of the earth, in the mountains of the moon, and in the farthest stars. The human ear isn't tuned to such a language, yet when a man listens with all his senses and his whole soul to God's speech, he may begin to understand a number of His words. The scientist tries to comprehend God's language and grammar through the medium of logic and experience. The mystic listens to God's voice within himself, his blood and marrow, and through observing the ways of Providence. The mystic finds that when he prays to God with great fervor, an answer often comes. He realizes that every gift of exaltation evolves after much doubt and a deep urge to unite with the higher powers. Hope grows from despair. The mystic often finds that doing good for people and even for animals brings results. Every true mystic believes in the immortality of the soul. The mystic cannot accept the notion that the soul is extinguished like the flame of a candle and that it vanishes forever. He generally doesn't believe in death. Like every other person, the mystic is brought up with the concept that there are good deeds and bad, acts of evil and sins, but it is harder for him than for any other person to accept the notion that the urge to do good and the urge to do bad both stem from the same source. The mystic must accept a certain form of dualism. He must recognize the presence of good forces and evil forces. He must believe that there is a God and an anti-God. True, the anti-God is not a completely independent entity—God had to create him for some purpose. All the mystics believe in Satan, or by whatever name he may be called.

Why did God create Satan? Why would the King of Heaven create an adversary for Himself? This is a question all religious thinkers and mystics have pondered through the ages, and although the answers seem to vary, often emerging tangled and obtuse or tightly bound up with folklore and magic, in essence the answer is always the same: God bestowed upon man the greatest gift in His treasury —free will, a certain autonomy. Man is not compelled in every instance to do what the Forces tell him. He can make a choice. He can oppose God or Satan and take upon himself the consequences of this resistance.

I don't propose in this essay to write the history of mysticism or even the history of Jewish mysticism. This has been done and is being done by scholars. This essay will try to relate the experiences of one who considers himself a bit of a mystic both in his life and in his literary creations. Whether this individual case merits a detailed description is something for the reader to judge. I believe myself to be the best authority to describe this particular story with all its uniqueness and—if you will—its peculiarities. I came from a Hasidic household and began early in life to probe into Hasidic and cabalistic lore as well as take an interest in what's called psychic research, and I will touch on these subjects as they relate to me and to my feelings about mysticism.

A Little Boy in Search of God

Mysticism in a Personal Light

1

Those who have read my works, particularly my autobiographical volume, *In My Father's Court,* know that I was born and reared in a house where religion, Jewishness, was virtually the air that we breathed. I stem from generations of rabbis, Hasidim, and cabalists. I can frankly say that in our house Jewishness wasn't some diluted formal religion but one that contained all the flavors, all the vitamins, the entire mysticism, of faith. Because the Jews had lived for two thousand years in exile, been driven from land to land and from ghetto to ghetto, their religion hadn't evaporated. The Jews underwent a selection the likes of which has no parallel in any of the other faiths. Those Jews lacking strong enough religious convictions or feelings fell to the wayside and assimilated with the gentiles. The only ones left were those who took their religion seriously and gave their children a full religious upbringing. The Diaspora Jew clung to only one hope—that the Messiah would come. Messiah's coming was not some worldly redemption, a recovery of lost territory, but a spiritual deliverance that would change the whole world, root out all evil, and bring the Kingdom of Heaven to earth.

In our house the coming of the Messiah was taken most literally. My younger brother, Moshe, and I often spoke about it. First, the sound of the ram's horn would be heard. It would be blown by the Prophet Elijah, and its sound would be heard round the world proclaiming the news: "Redemption came to the World! Salvation came to the World!" All the malefactors and enemies of Israel would perish leaving only the good gentiles whose privilege it would now become to serve the Jews. According to the Talmud, the Land of Israel would extend over all the nations. A fiery Temple would descend unto Jerusalem from heaven. The Kohanim, or priestly class (we were Kohanim), would offer sacrifices—possibly fiery sacrifices—because already then the slaughter of oxen, sheep, and turtledoves seemed to me not conducive to redemption. Abraham, Isaac, Jacob, and their tribes; Moses, King David, all the prophets, sages, geonim, and saints, would be resurrected along with the rest of the Jewish dead. My father had published a book in which there was a family tree tracing our descent from Shabatai Cohen, from Rabbi Moshe Isserlis, from Rashi, until King David. My brother Moshe and I would enter the palace where King David sat with crown on head on a golden throne and call him "Grandpa! . . ."

How poor seemed the gentiles with their kings, princes, soldiers, and wars in comparison with what awaited us! But in order to achieve all this, we had to be pious Jews,

study the Torah, do good deeds, pray with fervor, and obey our parents. . . .

All this would have been good and fine except that at an early age I already started asking myself: "Is it true?"

The only proof my parents could offer me was the holy books, which said that it would be so. But books were only paper and ink and written by people. I knew already that the gentiles had books, too, in which it was written that the Jews were a sinful race and that on Judgment Day they would be condemned to eternal damnation for having failed to accept Jesus. I also knew of heretical books which denied both Moses and Jesus. My brother Joshua, who was eleven years older than I (two girls in between had died of scarlet fever), often discussed this with my mother. These books claimed that the world was millions of years old, hundreds of millions. The people stemmed not from Adam, but from apes. God hadn't created the world in six days; the earth had torn away from the sun, and after taking millions of years to cool, it developed living creatures. Traces of ancient creatures were found in stones and in amber. Bones and horns were found of animals that had lived forty and fifty million years ago. Moses hadn't parted the Red Sea, Joshua hadn't stopped the sun in Gibeon, and the Messiah would never come. My brother spoke not of God's wonders, but of the wonders of nature. How mighty and magnificent nature was! There were stars whose light reached our

eyes after millions of years. Everything that existed—people, dogs, pigs, bedbugs, the sea, the rivers, the mountains, the moon—was part of this nature. But for all its greatness, nature was blind. It couldn't differentiate between good and evil. During an earthquake, saints perished along with sinners. The floods inundated synagogues and churches, the mansions of the rich and the shacks of the poor. The pious and the heretics both died during the epidemics. This nature had never begun and could never end. It followed its own laws. It was sand, rocks, electricity, light, fire, water. Our brains were part of this nature, too. Our heads thought, but nature did not. Our eyes saw and our ears heard, but nature was blind and deaf. It was no smarter than the cobblestone in the street or the refuse in the large garbage bin in our courtyard.

I recall a Sabbath in summer following the holiday meal. Mother and Father took a nap as was the custom on Sabbath day; my younger brother, Moshe, had gone down to play in the courtyard; my older brother, Joshua, had gone off somewhere to "those streets" where there were libraries with heretical books, museums, and theaters, and where students carried on affairs with rich, pretty, and educated girls. Who knows what sins my brother committed there? Maybe he rode the streetcar despite the Sabbath, handled money, or kissed a girl. According to the holy books I had studied, he would roast in hell or be reincarnated as an animal, a beetle, or maybe even as the sails of a windmill.

Joshua was already writing stories that he called literature and painting portraits. I went out onto our balcony—a boy with a pale face, blue eyes, and red earlocks—and I tried to think about the world. I pondered and at the same time observed what went on in the street below. The passers-by were as divided in their beliefs and attitudes as were the children in our house. Here, a bearded Jew with earlocks walked by in a fur-lined hat and satin gabardine—probably one of the Hasidim late after services—and soon a dandy came by in modern clothes, yellow shoes, a straw hat, clean-shaven and with a cigarette between his lips. He smoked openly on the Sabbath demonstrating his lack of faith in the Torah. Now came a pious young matron with a bonnet on her shaven head, to be closely followed by a girl with rouged cheeks, a kind of blue eye shadow, and a short-sleeved blouse that revealed her bare arms. She stopped to talk to the street loafers and even exchanged kisses with them. She carried a purse, even though this was forbidden on the Sabbath. A few years before, such boys and girls had tried to launch a revolution and overthrow the Tsar. They threw bombs and shot a grocer on Krochmalna Street for allegedly being a bourgeois. Some of the rebels had been hanged; others were in prison or exiled to Siberia. This crowd laughed at my father and his piety. They predicted that after the revolution there would be no more synagogues or study houses, and they called the Hasidim fanatics. Other young men and women on our street felt that the

Jews shouldn't wait for the Messiah but should themselves build up the Land of Israel, which they called Palestine. They argued that all peoples had their countries and that Jews being a people, too, needed a land of their own. The Messiah would never come on his donkey. Their leader, Dr. Herzl, had died the year I was born. There were also thieves on our street, gangsters, pimps, whores, fences who bought stolen goods. The fact was that not all the Hasidim were such honest people themselves. Some of them were known to be swindlers. They went bankrupt every few months and settled for a half or for a third with the manufacturers.

"What does all this mean?" I asked myself. "Wherein lies the truth? It must be somewhere, after all!"

At first glance, my brother Joshua seemed to be right. Nature demonstrated no religion. It didn't speak or preach. It apparently didn't concern nature that the slaughterers in Yanash's Market daily killed hundreds or thousands of fowl. Nor did it bother nature that the Russians made pogroms on Jews or that the Turks and Bulgarians massacred each other and carried little children on the tips of their bayonets. Well, but how had nature become that which it was? Where did it get the power to watch over the farthest stars and over the worms in the gutter? What were those eternal laws by which it acted? What was light? What was electricity? What went on deep inside the earth? Why was the sun so hot and so bright? And what was that

inside my head that had to be constantly thinking? At times Mother brought brains home from the market—brains were cheaper than beef. Mother cooked these brains and I ate them. Could my brains be cooked and eaten, too? Yes, of course, but so long as they weren't cooked, they kept on thinking and wanting to know the truth.

2

There were a number of holy books in my father's bookcase in which early in life I sought the answers to my questions. One was the *Book of the Covenant,* which I believe was already at that time a hundred years old and full of scientific facts. It described the theories of Copernicus and Newton and, it seems, the experiments of Benjamin Franklin as well. There were accounts of savage tribes, strange animals, and explanations of what made a train run and a balloon fly. In the special section dealing with religion were mentioned a number of philosophers. I recall that Kant already figured in there, too. The author, Reb Elijah of Vilna, a pious Jew, proved how inadequate the philosophers were at explaining the mystery of the world. No research or inquiry, wrote he, could reveal the truth. The author of the *Book of the Covenant* spoke of nature, too, but with the constant reminder that nature was something that God had created, not a thing that existed of its own power. I never tired of reading this book. Things had already evolved in my time of which the author of the *Book of the Covenant* could not know. In the delicatessen near our house there was a telephone. From time to time, a car drove down our street. My brother said that such rays had

been discovered that could photograph the heart and the lungs and that an instrument existed that revealed the stuff of which stars were made. The Yiddish newspaper read in our house often printed articles about Edison, the inventor of the phonograph. Each such account was for me like a treasure find. Because of my deep curiosity about science, I should have grown up a scientist, but I wasn't satisfied with mere facts—I wanted to solve the mystery of being. I sought answers to questions which tormented me then and still do to the present day.

The street was crowded with people, and our balcony swarmed with living creatures. Here came a butterfly and there a big fly with a green-gold belly; here landed a sparrow and suddenly a pigeon came swooping in from somewhere. An insect lighted on the lapel of my gabardine. In heder we called it Moses' little cow. Actually it was a ladybug. It was odd to consider that all these creatures had had fathers, mothers, grandfathers, and grandmothers just like me. Each of them lived out his or her time and died. I had read somewhere that a fly had thousands of eyes. Well, but despite all these eyes boys caught flies, tore off their wings, and tortured them in every manner only man could conceive while the Almighty sat on His Throne of Glory in seventh heaven and the angels sang His praises.

There were cabala books in my father's bookcase which intrigued me immensely. I was forbidden to study them. Father constantly reminded me that you couldn't take to the cabala before you reached thirty. He said that for those younger, the cabala posed a danger. One could drift into heresy and even lose one's mind, God forbid. When Father wasn't at home or was taking his Sabbath nap, I browsed through these books. They listed names of angels, seraphim. God's name was printed in large letters and in many variations. There were descriptions of heavenly mansions, transmigrated souls, spiritual copulations. The writers of these books were apparently well versed in the ways of heaven. They knew of combinations of letters through which you could tap wine from a wall, create pigeons, even destroy the world. Besides God Himself (there were no words or satisfactory terms to describe what He is), the one who had the main say above was Metatron, who ranked just a notch below God. A second mighty and awesome angel was Sandalphon. All the angels, seraphim, cherubim, had one desire—to praise God, to revere Him, to extol Him, to enhance His name. Their wings spread over the many worlds. They spoke Hebrew. I had learned in the Gemara that God understands all languages and that you could pray to Him in your own tongue, but the angels resorted only to Hebrew. Well, but this wasn't the same ordinary Hebrew that I knew. Holy names spurted from their fiery mouths, secrets of the Torah, mysteries upon mysteries. So vast were these heavens that three hundred and ten worlds were reserved for every saint. Every soul, big or small, the moment it passed the process of being cleansed in

fires of hell, found a place in Paradise—each according to its origin and its deeds. All the heavens, all the upper worlds, all the spheres, all the angels and souls, were concerned with one thing—to learn the secrets of the Torah, since God and the Torah and those who believed in the Torah, the Jews, were one and the same. . . . Every word, every letter, every curlicue, contained hints of Divine wisdom which no matter how often it was studied could never be learned, since, like God, the Torah was infinite. God Himself studied the Torah; that is to say, He studied His own depths. All the heavens, the entire eternity, were one great Yeshiva. God even found time to study with the souls of little children who had left the world early. In my imagination I pictured the Almighty sitting at a heavenly table surrounded by little souls in skullcaps and earlocks, all of them anxious to hear the word of Him for whom there wasn't sufficient praise to praise Him, nor enough knowledge to conceive Him, and of Whom the best thing that could be said was nothing.

Leafing through the cabala books, I discovered that even as they studied the Torah in the heavens, so did they indulge in fiery loves. In fact, in heaven Torah and love were two sides of the same coin. God coupled with the Divine Presence, which was actually God's wife, and the people of Israel were their children. When the Jews transgressed and God grew angry at them and wanted to punish them, the Divine Presence interceded for them like any Jewish

mother when the father is angry. The authors of the cabala books constantly warned against taking their writings literally. They were always afraid of anthropomorphism. Still, they did present a human concept. Not only God and the Divine Presence but all the male and female saints in the heavens loved one another and coupled both face to face and front to back.

Jacob again mated with Rachel, Leah, Bilhah, and Zilpah. The Patriarchs, King David, King Solomon, all the great people of the Scriptures and the Gemara, had wives and concubines in heaven. These couplings were unions performed for the glory of God. I already knew from reading the *Book of the Covenant* and maybe from glancing into my older brother's books that there were male trees and female trees. Winds and bees carried the pollen from one tree to another and fructified them. But I realized now that even in heaven the principle of male and female prevailed. I myself began to long for the mysteries of the girls in our street and courtyard. They seemed to eat, drink, and sleep just like men, but they looked different, spoke differently, smiled differently, dressed differently. Their lips, breasts, hips, throats, expressed something I didn't understand but was drawn to. The girls laughed at things that evoked no laughter in me. They thrilled over doodads that left me cold. They said words that struck me as silly and childish, yet their voices appealed to me. Not only God but also objects down here on earth had a language that defied interpretation. Hands, feet, eyes, noses—all had their own speech. They said something, but what? I had read somewhere that King Solomon understood the language of animals and birds. I had heard of people who could read faces and palms, and I yearned to know all this.

3

Some of the cabala books were chiefly concerned with sacred matters, but others, such as the *Book of Raziel* and the *Book of the Devout,* devoted much space to the powers of evil—demons, devils, imps, hobgoblins—as well as to magic. God had His kingdom, and Satan, or Asmodeus, had his own. The devil had secrets, too—dark secrets. The powers of goodness nourished themselves on the Torah and good deeds. They sought only to attain the truth, whereas the powers of darkness fed on lie, blasphemy, hate, envy, madness, cruelty. There were synagogues, houses of prayer, and Hasidic study houses on our street where Jews prayed, studied the Torah, and served God, but the street also contained taverns, brothels, and a den for thieves, pimps, and whores. There was a woman on the street of whom it was said that if she even glanced at a child she promptly gave it the evil eye. I knew her. A raging fire burned in her black eyes. It was said that three of her husbands had died and two had divorced her. She was capable of hitting a child she didn't know, tearing off his cap, or spitting at him. Every third word she uttered was a curse. She wore her own hair instead of a wig, but this wasn't hair but a kind of tangle of tufts, elflocks, and thorns. The

crooked eyes and wide nostrils brought to mind a bulldog. Her lips were thick, her teeth long, black, and as pointed as nails. My mother said that Satan gazed out of her eyes. She was allegedly a supplier of domestic help, but it was said that she induced country girls into prostitution and sold some of them into white slavery in a city far across the sea—Buenos Aires.

Because my brother Joshua had left the path of righteousness and denied both God and the devil, my parents often spoke of both these forces in order to overcome his arguments. If there were demons, there had to be a God. I heard countless stories of dybbuks, corpses that left their graves at night and wandered off to visit miracle workers or to attend distant fairs. Some of them forgot that they were dead and launched all kinds of business ventures or even got married. In Bilgoraj, my mother's home town, there was a ritual slaughterer, Avromele, on whose window an evil spirit had been beating for weeks on end. Every evening the whole population of the town gathered in the house to listen to the invisible force knock on the pane. One could discourse with it. One asked it questions and it tapped out the answers—mostly "yes" or "no" but occasionally entire words according to an agreed-upon code. The town *nachalnik,* a Russian, was apparently an enlightened man who didn't believe in evil spirits. He sent the police and soldiers to search the house—the attic, the cellar, every nook and cranny—to discover the source of the

noises, but they found nothing. Well, and what about the girl in Krasnik who was possessed by the soul of a sinful man which in a male voice recounted the sins and abominations he had committed during his lifetime? The girl was of common stock and didn't even know the alphabet, yet the dybbuk spouted passages and quotations from the Gemara, the Midrash, and other holy books. Often, wag that he was, he transposed the sacred words so that they emerged obscene but in a way apparent only to those who were learned. I read about such demons in storybooks. They were even mentioned in the Gemara, which spoke of Jewish demons and of gentile demons.

I lived in dread fear of these invisible beings. Our stairs were dark at night, and going up and down them became for me a terrible burden. I often counted the fringes on my ritual garment to see that none were missing. I mumbled incantations from the Gemara and from other sacred books. My brother Joshua laughed at me. He argued that there was no such thing as evil spirits. It was all fantasy, fanaticism. Well, but had a whole world conspired to make up the same lie? An anthology of German poetry had somehow found its way into our house. Since German is similar to Yiddish and because my eagerness to read was so great, I had learned to read German and I read Goethe's "Der Erlkönig," Heine's poem about the Lorelei, and many other mystical poems. The whole world believed in ghosts. If it could be shown that a piece of mud in the gutter housed millions of unseen microbes, why couldn't hordes of invisible ghosts be flying around in the air? Even my astute brother couldn't come up with an answer to this question.

There was a book in our house called *The Pillar of Service,* which explained the cabala in simpler terms. It claimed that God had existed forever. The author, Reb Baruch Kossover, "proved" the existence of God using the same arguments I found years later in Spinoza's *Ethics* and in other philosophical works. God's essence and His existence are identical. When we say that one and one makes two or that the sum of the angles in a triangle equals two right angles, we don't need a wooden triangle or two groschen to prove us right. One and one would equal two even if there were no objects in the world.

Once Reb Baruch Kossover had reassured the reader that there is a God, he went on to describe Him without any further proofs. Before God had created the world, all His traits or qualities had been completely merged within Him. Wisdom blended with mercy, beauty with strength, perpetuity with understanding and love. But it seemed that the urge to create was one of God's attributes, too. How could there be a king without a people? How could one be merciful when there wasn't anyone to receive the mercy? How could God love when there was no one to be loved? So long as God didn't create the world, all His traits were latent, not realized—potential, not factual. God needed a world, many

worlds, to become what He was. Creativeness was God's most obvious attribute.

But how could He create the world when He Himself and His radiance flooded everything? The answer given by the cabala, especially by Rabbi Isaac Lurie, is that in order to be able to create and to make room for Creation, God had to shrink or reduce Himself. It lay within His power—if He so desired—to dim or even extinguish part of His light. In the midst of the infinity He created a vacuum, where the Creation would come into being. Rabbi Baruch Kossover constantly warned the reader not to take him literally. God wasn't matter, and the emptiness He created wasn't one of space but one of quality. When a teacher taught a child just entering heder, he wouldn't try to make him grasp the intricacies of the Talmud or the commentaries. The teacher had, in a sense, to compress his thinking in order to adjust it to the capacities of his young pupil. According to the cabala, Creation was a process of diminution and emanation. First God created the World of Emanation. This world was still close to God, as spiritually elevated as can be conceived, but even *it* already revealed God's traits or *sephiroth*: the Crown, Wisdom, Understanding, Mercy, Power, Splendor, Infinity, Magnificence, Fundamentality, Kingdom. This spiritually exalted world then emanated a world that was lower, the World of Creation, which possessed the same ten *sephiroth*. Later came the World of Form,

and only then the World of Deed or the World of Matter, with all the stars, galaxies, comets, planets; and, it seems, at the very end was created our world. Actually, we were all part of God's light, but through the process of emanation and diminution God's light grew ever darker, ever more specific and accessible, until it turned into matter—earth, rocks, sea, animals, people. According to the cabala, Creation was a kind of gradual revelation and popularization of divinity. The cabala is pantheistic. My later interest in Spinoza stemmed from trying to study the cabala.

4

Although I was still young when I began to browse through the cabala books, I realized that their particulars weren't as important as was their concept that everything is God and God is everything; that the stone in the street, the mouse in its hole, the fly on the wall, and the shoes on my feet were all fashioned from the Divinity. The stone, I told myself, might appear dead, mute, cold, indifferent to good and evil, but somewhere deep within it, it was alive, knowledgeable, on the side of justice, united with God from Whose substance it was kneaded. Matter was a mask over the face of spirit. Behind smallness hid bigness, stupidity was crippled wisdom, evil was perverted mercy. Years later when I read that a stone consisted of trillions of molecules constantly in motion and that these molecules consisted of atoms and that these atoms were in themselves complicated systems, whirls of energy, I said to myself: "That's the cabala, after all!" Even as a boy I had heard that atoms were not merely dead balls of matter. Certain atoms such as radium emitted rays of light and energy for hundreds of years. I had heard the words "proton" and "electron." Slivers of scientific knowledge found their way into our pious household through the

newspapers and the Yiddish and Hebrew books my brother brought home. Science, just like the cabala, spoke of light that could be seen with human eyes and of invisible light. I had read somewhere about the ether that filled the endless space and whose vibrations allowed eyes to see, trees to grow, creatures to live and love. Later, I read that certain scholars denied the existence of this all-encompassing ether. There were heretics in science, too. There, too, they served an idol one day, and the next they dragged him through the slime. . . .

I existed on several levels. I was a heder boy, yet I probed the eternal questions. I asked a question about the Gemara and tried to explain the mysteries of Zeno. I studied the cabala and I went down to play tag and hide-and-seek with the boys in the courtyard. A woman named Bashele lived in our courtyard. She had a daughter my age called Shosha. Shosha and I played with broken spoons, with brass buttons, with shards and toys like little children. I was aware of being quite different from all the other boys, and I was deeply ashamed of this fact. Simultaneously I read Dostoevski in Yiddish translation and penny dreadfuls that I bought on Twarda Street for a kopeck. I suffered deep crises, was subject to hallucinations. My dreams were filled with demons, ghosts, devils, corpses. Sometimes before falling asleep I saw shapes. They danced around my bed, hovered in the air. In my fantasies or daydreams I brought the Messiah or was myself the Messiah. By utter-

ing magic words, I built a palace on a mountaintop in the Land of Israel or in the desert region, and I lived there with Shosha. Angels and demons served me. I flew to the farthest stars. I discovered a potion which when drunk revealed all the world's wisdom and made one immortal. I spoke with God and He disclosed His secrets to me.

My moods varied swiftly. Now I was in ecstasy and soon deep in despair. The cause of my gloom was often the same—unbearable pity for those who were suffering and who had suffered in all the generations. I had heard about the cruelties perpetrated by Chmielnicki's Cossacks. I had read about the Inquisition. I knew about the pogroms on Jews in Russia and Spain. I lived in a world of cruelty. I was tormented not only by the sufferings of men but by the sufferings of beasts, birds, and insects as well. Hungry wolves attacked lambs. Lions, tigers, and leopards had to devour other creatures or die from hunger. The squires wandered through forests and shot deer, hares, and pheasants for pleasure. I bore resentment not only against man but against God, too. It was He who had provided the savage beasts with claws and fangs. It was He who had made man a bloodthirsty creature ready to do violence at every step. I was a child, but I had the same view of the world that I have today—one huge slaughterhouse, one enormous hell. My brother had brought home a brochure about Darwin which contained a chapter about Malthus. Making sure my father shouldn't see me, I read the book in a single

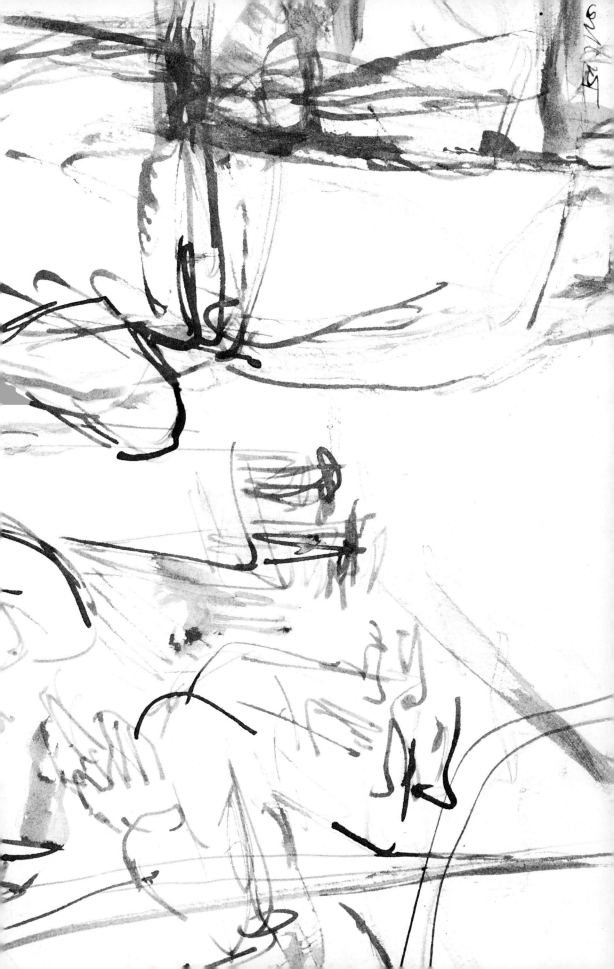

day. Malthus proved in a way that couldn't be clearer that countless creatures were born to die, for otherwise the world would fill with so many creatures that everyone would starve to death or simply become crushed. Wars, plagues, and famines sustained life on this earth. Darwin went even further and maintained that the continuous struggle for food or sex is the origin of all species. The Cossacks who massacred the Jews, the Russians, the Tartars, all the tribes that kept on killing each other, actually implemented the plans of Creation. Kill or be killed was the rule of life and of God. Malthus' contentions denied all the claims of the Scriptures that God despised bloodshed. Actually He had so constructed the world that blood should spill, that children should starve to death, that beasts should devour each other. I read these truths that I knew no one could deny, yet at the same time I felt as if I were swallowing poison. I closed this terrible book and began to browse through the Scriptures. I had long been aware of the amazing contradictions contained in this holy volume. The same Moses who said, "Thou shalt not kill" also said, "Thou shalt save alive nothing that breatheth." The wars waged by Joshua bore an uncanny resemblance to the outrages perpetrated by Chmielnicki's Cossacks. King David, the alleged author of the Psalms, hardly conducted himself like a psalmist should. Before my eyes the vision had long lingered of how he measured prisoners with a rope to indicate which would live and which would die. Since a mur-

derer was a malefactor, how could King David be called a saint? And why must the Messiah descend from King David? And when the Messiah came, how would I be able to call King David, a murderer, "Grandpa"? In the Psalms it said that people of violence and falseness are an abomination to God. Well, but how could God abominate them if they carried out His bids?

No, I could find no answer in the Scriptures. The Scriptures indirectly confirmed the theories of Malthus. When the Jews were stronger, they killed the Philistines, and when the Philistines were stronger, they killed the Jews. According to the Scriptures, the Jews fell before their foe because they had sinned, but was every soldier in the war a sinner? And what about the children who were frequent victims of these wars? It seemed that God didn't punish individual sinners directly—He punished the entire group. But this same God had also said that fathers mustn't die for the sins of their children nor children for the sins of the fathers, but that everyone must die for his own sins.

I did find a trace of comfort in the cabala books. These books described the earth as the meanest of all the worlds. The evil spirits, the dissenters, Satan, Lilith, Naamah, Machlat, Shibta—all had dominion in this den of evil. Our world was the lowest of all the worlds, far removed from God and His mercy. But just because we were so far from God and His benevolence, He had given us the greatest gift in His treasury—free will. The angels have no choice, but

man could choose between good and evil. This world is, you might say, the weakest link in God's chain, and a chain is only as strong as its weakest link. When man chooses virtue, he strengthens all the spheres. Angels and seraphim look forward to a man doing a good deed, since this brings joy and strength to all the worlds. A good deed helps God and the Divine Presence to unite. A sin, on the other hand, evokes gloom in all the worlds.

Assume it was so. But does a cat have a choice? Does a mouse? I once heard the scream of a mouse that a cat had caught, and this cry haunts me still. Do the chickens slaughtered in Yanash's Market have a choice? Do they have to suffer because of *our* choice? Well, and those children that died of scarlet fever, diphtheria, whooping cough, and other diseases—how were they guilty? I had read and heard that the souls of the dead were resurrected in cattle and fowl and that when the slaughterer killed them with a kosher knife and said the blessing with fervor, this served to purify these souls. What about those cows and hens that fell into the hands of gentile butchers? . . .

"I'm becoming a heretic!" I said to myself, or thought it.

My urge to know what the unbelievers or the scientists had to say grew ever stronger. Who knows—perhaps the truth lies with them? A Jewish publisher in Warsaw had begun to issue a series of popular books on science, and I asked my brother to bring them to me. My brother and I now shared a secret. I read a popular book on physics. I read about astronomy. To the scientists, the universe was not smaller than the World of Deed as described in the cabala. In infinite space floated countless bodies, some already cooled, others of a temperature of thousands and millions of degrees, others still composed of gases or mists. All these bodies were ruled by one law—gravity. The book provided the cosmological theory of Kant and Laplace. Earlier, the universe had consisted of one immense fog. This fog existed in a state of equilibrium. But something occurred so that in one place in this fog the molecules grew denser and began to attract the surrounding molecules. A body formed which grew from moment to moment—a cosmic ball. In time, this ball grew so immense that it tore apart and formed the sun, the other stars, the planets, and the comets. The sun itself grew too big and unwieldly so that a part of it tore away and later became our earth and the moon. . . . I discussed this theory with my brother. "Where did the first fog come from?" I asked him, and my brother replied: "Where did God come from? You must accept the fact that something has existed forever and you can just as well say that nature existed forever as you can say that God did. It's the same with gravity and all the other laws. They were a part of nature forever, but so long as the cosmic fog was in a state of equilibrium these laws remained passive (more or less)."

Even a child could detect the similarity between the cabala and the cosmology of Kant and Laplace. The only difference lay in that the infinity as described by the cabala possessed consciousness, wisdom, beauty, and mercy, whereas the fog of Kant and Laplace was a dead golem. To the question of how this dead golem could have produced trees, blossoms, birds, lions, Maimonides, Copernicus, Newton, and the Baal Shem, the scientists had one answer: development, evolution. My father called it by another name—an inkwell that had spilled on a scroll three miles long and written a book full of wisdom. . . .

In the midst of all this, World War I erupted. Some assassin had killed the Austrian archduke and his wife, and millions of soldiers and civilians had to pay with their lives for this crime. The scholars of all the nations harnessed the eternal laws to decimate the enemy peoples. The Jews in the Radzymin study house where my father worshiped (we had moved from number 10 to number 12 Krochmalna Street) said that there were such cannons now that could kill a thousand soldiers with one shot. The airplane had been invented, a kind of heavier-than-air balloon. Until the war we had to be careful with the Yiddish newspaper in our house. Father said that the newspapers were full of blasphemy and heresy. He said that to start the day by reading the paper was like eating poison for breakfast. But as the armies fought around the towns and villages where we came from and the Tsar's uncle, Nikolai Nikolaevich, ordered the Jews driven out of those towns and even took Jews as hostage and sent them to Siberia, Father started to

glance into the papers, too—not the first thing in the morning but later in the day, after praying and studying. New words had emerged which Father had never before heard. The Jew who had been in exile for two thousand years and never mixed into the gentile wars had almost no names for arms and ammunition. Nor did he have words for strategy and tactics. The Yiddish journalists had to adapt all these words from the German and occasionally from Russian and Polish. Father read the reports. The enemy (the Germans) was constantly being repulsed—still he kept advancing steadily despite the heavy losses. The numbers of dead and wounded were listed. At times the writer added: "We suffered heavy casualties, too." Father gripped his red beard while his blue eyes gazed out the window and up to heaven. They fought and shed blood over some poverty-stricken village, some muddy stream. They burned the wooden shacks and the meager possessions of paupers who often had to flee into the cold nights with their children. I heard Father mumble: "Woe, woe is us, God in heaven!"

I wanted to say: "Papa, this isn't the fault of God but of evolution. Had the fog remained in a state of equilibrium, we would all be in peace."

5

We starved at home. Bitter frosts raged outside, but our stove wasn't lit. Mother lay in bed all day and read her books of morals—*Duty of the Heart, The Rod of Punishment, The Good Heart,* and occasionally the aforementioned *Book of the Covenant.* Her face was white and bloodless. She, too, sought the answers to the eternal questions, but her faith remained firm. She didn't cast a speck of doubt upon the Almighty. Mother argued with my older brother: "It isn't the Creator's fault. He wanted to give the Torah to Esau and Ishmael but they rejected it." My brother asked: "Were you there?" He denied the concept of free choice. There was no such thing as free will. If you were born into a Jewish house, you believed in Jewishness; if you were born into a Christian home, you believed in Jesus; if you were born a Turk, you believed in Mohammed. He said to Mother: "If someone abducted you as a child out of your father's house and raised you among gentiles, you'd keep on crossing yourself, and instead of the pious books you'd be reading the history of the Christian martyrs now."

Mother grimaced at this blasphemy and said: "May the Almighty forgive your words."

"There is no Almighty. Man is an animal like all animals. This whole war is on account of oil."

This was the first time I had ever heard such words. Oil, of all things? All the time we had lived in number 10 we had used oil in our lamps. Now that we lived in number 12 we used gas. It seemed incredible to me that Germany, Russia, England, and France should fight over such a filthy thing as oil, but my brother soon explained it.

Mother heard him out and said: "They only need an excuse to fight. Today they fight over oil; tomorrow it'll be over soap or cream of tartar. The fact is that they are evildoers and the evildoer must commit evil. All he needs is an excuse."

"When the Jews had a country, they fought, too. The whole notion of the 'chosen people' isn't worth a row of beans. We're the same animals as all the others. We have our share of swindlers, fakers, and charlatans."

"It's all because of the accursed exile."

I didn't know myself with whom to agree—I loved them both deeply—but it appeared that my brother was right. Whatever home one was raised in, that was the faith one accepted. The home hypnotized people like that hypnotist Feldman described in the newspapers. That which Feldman did in a minute the home did gradually. If you heard day in and day out that there is a God, you believed in God. If you raised children to believe that everything resulted from evolution, they would believe in evolution. But which

was the truth? I, Itchele from number 12 Krochmalna Street, wouldn't let myself be hypnotized by anybody. I had to consider everything on my own and come to my own conclusions! I realized by now that reading popular books on science wouldn't reveal the secret of the world to me. Kant and Laplace were men, too, not angels. How could they possibly know what had happened millions and myriads of years ago? Since one cannot dig a pit seven miles deep and see what goes on beneath the earth, how could they know how the universe had formed? It was all supposition or plain guesswork. Both the cabala and the astronomy book spoke of presences that existed forever, but I couldn't for the life of me conceive of such a thing. If God or the fog had existed forever, this would mean you could take a wagonful of pencils and write the number of years these presences had existed and it still wouldn't be enough. The fact was that you couldn't write this total with all the pencils in the world on all the paper in the world. In the book on astronomy it stated that space was without limit as was the number of heavenly bodies. But how could something stretch on without an end? On the other hand, how could time have a beginning? What was *before* the beginning? And how could space have a limit? I spoke of this to my brother, and he said: "Your questions have to do with philosophy, not with science, but you can't find the truth there either."

"Where can you find it?"

"The real truth was never known, it isn't known, and it will never be known. Just like a fly can't pull a wagon of coal or iron, our brain can't fathom the truth of the world."

"In that case, what's to be done?"

"Eat, drink, sleep, and if it's possible, try to create a better order."

"What kind of order?"

"One in which the nations stop slaughtering each other and people have work, food, and a decent place to live."

"How can this be done?"

"Oh, there are all kinds of theories."

My brother waved his hand. He himself was in deep trouble. He was hiding from the Russian military authorities. He lived under a false passport listing a different name and different place of birth. He was living in some unheated studio of a sculptor and starving along with the rest of us. He risked his life every moment, since deserters were shot. Mother cried her eyes out as she prayed to God that no harm befall him. Although I doubted the existence of God, I, too, prayed to Him (whenever I forgot that I was a heretic). After all, you couldn't be sure about such things.

My brother left, but before leaving, he glanced out the window to see if the "coast was clear"—that no military patrols were roaming about. I began to pace to and fro like a caged beast. How could you live in such a world? How could you breathe when you were condemned to never, never know where you came from, who you were, where

you were going? I looked out the window and saw a freight wagon of sacks drawn by a skinny nag. I compared myself to this creature that pulled a load without knowing what it was or where it was going or why it had to strain so. My brother had just now advised me, like Ecclesiastes, to eat, drink, and sleep, but I had nothing to eat and it wasn't even easy to drink a glass of water, since our water pipes had frozen. No matter how I covered myself at night I still felt cold. The mice in our apartment were apparently starving, too, since they grew ever bolder in their desperation—they even leaped over our beds. Well, and how would I go about creating a better order? Should I write a letter to Nicholas II or to Wilhelm II or to the English King that it didn't pay to go to war over oil? Hadn't Malthus said that wars and epidemics were useful—actually vital to man's existence?

My brother had mentioned the philosophers, and although he said that I could learn nothing from them, they had to know something, after all. Otherwise, why were they called philosophers? But where did one get such a book? I could have asked my brother, but first of all, he seldom came home now, and secondly, he often forgot what I asked him for and it took him weeks to remember. But I had to learn the answer right now! I began to rummage among my brother's papers, and I found what I wanted—a book from Bresler's Library listing its address somewhere on Nowolipki Street. Now I was ready to launch the biggest adventure of my life—namely, I resolved to go to

this library and try to get a book out on philosophy. It was my feeling that my brother had probably already read this book and that it was high time he brought it back. A few times cards had come from the library demanding from my brother that he bring back books that were overdue. I would therefore take this book back and ask for another in its stead, one on philosophy. It was true that if my brother found out what I had done, he might grow terribly angry and might even slap me for going where I didn't belong. But what was a slap compared to the joy that a book on philosophy would grant me? I burned with the urge to read what the philosophers had to say about God, the world, time, space, and, most of all, why people and animals must suffer so. This to me was the question of questions.

I took the book and started off toward Nowolipki Street. It was freezing outside. The Germans had pushed so close to Warsaw that I could hear their cannonfire in the streets. I pictured to myself how a thousand soldiers died from every shot. Freezing blasts blew, making my nose feel like a piece of wood. I had no gloves, and the fingers of the hand holding the book had become stiff. I was terribly afraid they would yell at me at the library or make fun of me. Who knows? My brother might even be there. I raced against the wind, and a voice within me shouted, "I must learn the truth! Once and for all!"

I went inside the library and, for a moment, saw nothing. My eyes grew bedazzled and my head spun. "If only I

don't faint!" I prayed to the forces that guided the world. Gradually the dizziness subsided, and I saw a huge room, actually a hall stacked with books from floor to the astoundingly high ceiling. The sun shone in through the windows casting a bright wintery light. Behind a wide counter stood a corpulent man—bareheaded, beardless, with longish hair and a mustache—who placed paper patches on the margins of a book. For a long time he didn't look up, then he noticed me, and his big black eyes expressed a kind of amiable surprise.

He said: "What do you say, young fellow?"

I savored the title "young fellow." It was a sign that I was already half grown.

I replied: "I brought back my brother's book."

The librarian stuck out his hand and took the book. He stared for a long time at the inside of the cover and knitted his brow. Then he asked: "Israel Joshua Singer is your brother?"

"Yes, my older brother," I replied.

"What's happened to him? It's a year since he took out this book. You're not allowed to keep a book longer than a month. A pretty big fine has accumulated. More than the deposit."

"My brother is in the Army," I said, astounded over my own lie. It was obviously either my way of justifying my brother's failure to return the book or a means of drawing sympathy to myself. The librarian shook his head.

"Where is he—in the war?"

"Yes, the war."

"You don't hear from him?"

"Not a word."

The librarian grimaced.

"What do they want—those savages? Why do they drag innocent victims into their murderous wars?" He spoke half to me, half to himself. He paused a moment, then said: "Your brother is a talented young man. He writes well. He paints well, too. A talent. A born talent. Well, and you obviously study at the study house, eh?"

"Yes, I study, but I want to know what goes on in the world, too," I said. I had the feeling that my mouth was speaking of its own volition.

"Oh? What do you want to know?"

"Oh—physics, geography, philosophy—everything."

"Everything, eh? No one knows everything."

"I want to know the secret of life," I said, ashamed of my own words. "I want to read a book on philosophy."

The librarian arched his brows.

"What book? In what language?"

"In Yiddish. I understand Hebrew, too."

"You mean, the sacred language?"

"My brother read the *Ha-tzephirah,* and I read it, too."

"And your father let you read such a heretical paper?"

"He didn't see."

The librarian mulled this over.

"I have something about philosophy in Yiddish, but a boy your age should study useful things, not philosophy. It'll be difficult for you and it'll serve no practical purpose."

"I want to know what the philosophers say about why people must suffer and how the world came about."

"The philosophers don't know this themselves. Wait here."

He went to search among the books and even climbed a ladder. He came down with two books and showed them to me. One was in Yiddish, the other in Hebrew.

He said: "I have something for you, but if your father should see them, he'd tear them to pieces."

"My father won't see them. I'll hide them well."

"When you take out books from a library, you have to leave a deposit and pay for a month in advance, but you probably haven't a groschen. All right, I'll take the chance, but bring them back when you're finished. And keep them clean. If you bring them back in time, I'll find something else for you. If a boy wants to learn the secret of life, you have to accommodate him."

The librarian smiled and marked something down on cards. He handed me the books, and I barely restrained myself from kissing his hand. A great surge of affection swept over me toward this good person along with the desperate urge to read what was written in these books.

6

I finished the Yiddish book that same day. I became so engrossed in it I even forgot my hunger. There were only a few pages devoted to most philosophers in this book. Some of them—Plato, Aristotle, and Democritus—were familiar to me from browsing through *Guide to the Perplexed, The Khuzari,* and *Faiths and Opinions* and other volumes in our house as well as the *Book of the Covenant*. I understood only a little of what I read, but I plowed right through lest my father catch me, tear these heretical books to pieces, and slap me besides. I was anxious to discover as quickly as possible why men and animals had to suffer. The philosophers offered various opinions regarding the creation of the world, but I clung to the question "How do they know?" Since they weren't in heaven, and neither God nor the First Cause nor the Entelechy spoke to them, how could I reply on them? I encountered such words as idea, form, categories, substance, monads, idealism, materialism, empiricism, solipsism, but the questions of how things could exist forever, how the world could be without limit, and why cats caught mice remained unanswered. Only one philosopher, Schopenhauer, mentioned the sufferings of men and animals, but according to this book, he offered no explanations for it. The world, he said, consisted of a blind will, of passions that had no reason and that the intellect served them like a slave. . . .

After a while, I turned to the Hebrew book. Reading about philosophy in Hebrew was even harder for me than in Yiddish. Actually I didn't read but scanned through the pages for parts that would answer my questions in clear fashion, but there was less clarity here than in the books on the cabala, particularly *The Pillar of Service*. The pleasure that I got from these two books gradually turned into despair and rage. If the philosophers didn't know and couldn't know—as Locke, Hume, and Kant themselves indicated—what need was there for all those high-flown words? Why all the research? I had the suspicion that the philosophers pretended, masked their ignorance behind Latin and Greek phrases. Besides, it seemed to me that they skirted the main issues, the essence of things. The question of questions was the suffering of creatures, man's cruelty to man and to animals. Even if it provided answers to all the other questions but this one, philosophy would still be worthless.

Those were my feelings then, and those are my feelings still. But in reading about these philosophers I got the impression that the question of suffering was of little consequence to them.

My brother had left a dictionary of foreign words and phrases in the house, and I looked up the more difficult words. On one page of one of the philosophy books it discussed whether the sentence "Seven and five equals twelve" is *a priori* or synthetically *a priori*. I looked up the meaning of *a priori* and "synthetic" as well as of "analytic," which was mentioned there, too, and at the same time I thought: "How can it help the chewed-up mouse or the devoured lamb whether the sentence 'Seven and five equals twelve,' is analytic or synthetic?" I know today that the whole Kantian philosophy hangs on this question, but the problem of problems is still to me the suffering of people and animals. I have the same feeling today when I try to read the convoluted commentaries of Wittgenstein and his disciples who try to convince themselves and others that all that we lack is a clear definition of words. Give us a dictionary with crystal-clear definitions (if such a thing is even possible) and the pains of all the martyrs of all times and of all the tortured creatures would become justified forever. . . .

In the course of the month that I kept the two books (I don't know to this day who their authors were) I read them virtually day and night. I constantly referred to the dictionary, but the more I read and probed in these books, the more obvious it became to me that I would find no answers to my questions in them. Actually, the philosophers all said the same thing I had heard from my mother—that the ways of God (or of nature or of Substance or of the Absolute) were hidden. We didn't know them and we couldn't know.

Even then I detected the similarity between the cabala and Baruch Spinoza. Both felt that everything in the world is a part of God, but while the cabala rendered to God such attributes as will, wisdom, grandeur, mercy, Spinoza attributed to God merely the capacity to extend and to think. The anguish of people and animals did not concern Spinoza's God even in the slightest. He had no feelings at all concerning justice or freedom. He Himself wasn't free but had to act according to eternal laws. The Baal Shem and the murderer were of equal importance to Him. Everything was preordained, and no change whatsoever could affect Spinoza's God or the things that were part of Him. Billions of years ago He knew that someone would assassinate the Austrian archduke and that Nikolai Nikolaevich would have an old rabbi in a small Polish town hanged for being an alleged German spy.

The book said that Spinoza proposed that God be loved with a rational love (*amor Dei intellectualis*), but how could you love such a mighty and wise God who didn't possess even a spark of compassion toward the tortured and beaten? This philosophy exuded a chill, though still I felt that it might contain more truth (bitter truth) than the cabala. If God were indeed full of mercy and benevolence, He wouldn't have allowed starvation, plagues, and pogroms. Spinoza's God merely fortified the contentions of Malthus.

When the Germans entered Warsaw, the hunger be-

came even worse. An epidemic of typhus broke out. My younger brother, Moshe, caught the spotted typhus and was taken to the municipal hospital. His life was in danger, and Mother cried her eyes out begging God (or whoever was in charge) in his behalf. Spinoza taught me that prayers couldn't help in any way, but the cabala books said that prayers recited with fervor went straight to the Throne of Glory and could avert the worst decree. How could Spinoza be so sure that God had no will or compassion? He, Spinoza, was no more than blood and flesh himself, after all. Thank God, Moshe recovered.

Between 1915 and 1917, hundreds of people died on Krochmalna Street. Now a funeral procession passed our windows and now the ambulance taking the sick to the hospital. I saw women shake their fists at the sky and in their rage call God a murderer and a villain. I saw Hasidim at the Radzymin study house and in the other study houses grow swollen from malnutrition. At home we ate frozen potatoes that had a sweetish, nauseating taste. The Germans kept scoring victories, but those who foretold that the war wouldn't last longer than six weeks had to admit their error. Millions of people had already perished, but Malthus' God still hadn't had enough.

In the midst of all this, the Revolution broke out in Russia. The Tsar was overthrown, and the Jews in the Radzymin study house promptly began to say that this was an omen presaging the coming of the Messiah. The dead rot-

ted, but new hopes were aroused in those still living. It was clear that this Revolution was an act of Providence, but the hunger and sicknesses in Warsaw grew steadily worse. Father became so dejected by the situation that he just about stopped paying attention to me, and I was free to read all the books I could get my hands on. Nor did I neglect to study the Gemara and the commentaries. I studied, read, and let my imagination soar. Since both the cabalists and the philosophers made everything up out of their heads, why couldn't I ferret the truth out with my own brain? Maybe it was destined that *I* should uncover the truth of Creation? But all my ruminations came smack up against the exasperating enigma of eternity and infinity and against the even deeper mystery of suffering and cruelty.

7

In the summer of 1917 my mother took me and my younger brother, Moshe, to Bilgoraj where her father had been the town rabbi for forty years. He had fled from the Russians to Lublin and had died there of the cholera. My grandmother Hannah was no longer living either. My uncle Joseph, Mother's brother, had become the Bilgoraj rabbi. I have described this trip in detail in my book *In My Father's Court*. The library in Bilgoraj was a small one, but I had already started reading Polish then, and I also had the opportunity to read the history of philosophy as well as Spinoza's *Ethics* in German. I even read Karl Marx's *Das Kapital* in Yiddish. Materialism—historical materialism particularly—never attracted me. In my worst moments of doubt I knew that this world hadn't evolved on its own but that behind it lay some plan, a consciousness, a metaphysical force. Blind forces couldn't create even one fly. But in Spinoza's *Ethics* I found a kind of cheerless greatness. Since according to Spinoza substance possessed an endless number of attributes, this left some room for fantasy. I even toyed with the notion of changing some of Spinoza's axioms and definitions and bringing out a new *Ethics*. You could easily say that time was one of God's at-

tributes, too, as well as purpose, creativeness, and growth. I had read somewhere about Lobachevski's non-Euclidian geometry, and I wanted to create a non-Spinozian pantheism, or whatever it might be called. I was ready to make will a divine attribute, too. This kind of revisionist Spinozism would come very close to the cabala.

There was an enlightened Jew in Bilgoraj, Todros the watchmaker, who took an interest in science and philosophy. I tutored his daughter—a beautiful girl—in Hebrew, and her father and I discussed the loftier matters. He subscribed to several scientific periodicals from Warsaw, and I learned from him about Einstein, Planck, and the fact that the atom was a kind of solar system with electrically positive protons and electrically negative electrons. The indivisibility of the atom had always puzzled me. No matter how small a thing was, you could always imagine a half of it, a quarter of it, and so on ad infinitum. I said to Todros in a Gemara chant: "Since the atom is not the final measure of smallness, why should it be the electron? A few years hence scholars will probably discover that the electron can be split, too, that it also consists of a system, and so on without an end. If bigness has no limit, then neither has smallness. It's altogether possible that each atom is a universe and that the electron is actually a planet inhabited by tiny people and animals. It's not inconceivable that on one of these planets sit an Isaac and Todros carrying on more or less the same discussion as we are."

A half-burned match lay on the table, and I said: "Nor is it inconceivable that this match contains countless worlds where people study, learn, marry, and breed—that there are universities there and philosophers writing books."

I wanted to add that there were loves there, too, since I was in love with his daughter, my pupil. Todros smiled and gazed at the match stub.

I went on: "Maybe our world is also part of some cosmic match. Maybe there exist such persons in the infinite universe who could stick our solar system in their pocket, and maybe they actually do this without our knowledge. . . ."

"Well, well, the things that all *could* be. . . . Science speaks only of things known to exist, not of the possibilities."

"I read that there are such rays that vibrate a million times a second. Maybe there are creatures, too, that can experience in one second what we experience in a hundred years."

"Yes, maybe. But meanwhile the situation on our planet grows ever worse. In the Ukraine they're slaughtering Jewish children like in Chmielnicki's times. I got a bunch of newspapers from Warsaw yesterday. It's hard to believe that such savageries are being committed in the twentieth century."

"The same savageries will be committed in the thirtieth century, in the fiftieth century, and in the hundredth century."

"Why do you say this, eh? Don't you believe in progress?"

"God wants murder—He must have it," I said. "Did you ever hear of Malthus?"

"Yes, I've heard of him and I've read him. But you can control human birth. French women have only two children. If people would stop breeding like rabbits, you wouldn't need all the wars and epidemics. In the civilized countries they've just about eliminated cholera. Typhus is rare there. Even here, smallpox is becoming extinct. You can regulate everything with knowledge and patience."

"If they will eliminate one sickness, others will crop up. God is evil," I said, astounded at my own words. "A good God wouldn't arrange it that wolves should devour lambs and cats should catch innocent mice."

"He is neither evil nor good," Todros said. "He doesn't exist and that's all there is to it. And nature doesn't care about morality."

"Where did nature come from?"

"Where did God come from? Nature is here and we must come to terms with it and use its laws for the good of humanity."

"What about the animals?"

"We can't worry about the animals."

The wick in the kerosene lamp cast a bright glow; the stove gave off warmth. My pupil brought two glasses of tea from the kitchen. Her face was pale, but her eyes were coal-black. She listened to our conversation and smiled. Girls never discussed such matters. They talked about shoes, dresses, engagements, weddings, and bargains you could pick up in the market. . . .

My new friend, Notte Schwerdscharf, made speeches and proposed that the Jews go to Palestine, but the girls didn't take him seriously. What difference did it make what Notte said anyway? Each Monday and Thursday he got a new crazy notion. There were already communists in Bilgoraj, too. There was even one Jewish youth who was a Polish patriot and had enlisted in Pilsudski's Legion. The pious Jews had organized an Orthodox party.

When my mother took me and my brother Moshe to Bilgoraj, my brother Joshua remained in Warsaw. He hadn't the slightest desire to bury himself away in such a God-forsaken hole as Bilgoraj. My father went back to Radzymin to help the Hasidic rabbi there compose his books. The Radzymin rabbi had a poor handwriting, and his spelling in Hebrew was atrocious. His commentaries were fatuous, and the scholars scoffed at him. The rabbi needed a "wet nurse," and my father fulfilled this capacity. Eventually, my brother went to Kiev, which the Germans had occupied, and he worked there in the local Yiddish press.

Later came the Bolshevik Revolution and with it, the bands that committed pogroms. Long months went by that we didn't hear from my brother. My sister Hindele had been living in Antwerp with her husband, and when the

Germans invaded Belgium, the couple fled to England. He being a Russian citizen, the English authorities sent him back to Russia to report for military duty. However, the Revolution had broken out in the meantime and he was stuck in Russia. My sister lived with a child in London without any means of support. The mails didn't function between England and Poland. For all these problems Mother had but one solution—praying. Compared to us, Todros lived in luxury and it was peaceful there. Todros' wife had a candy store which stayed open until late. I drank the tea, nibbled along on a cookie, and discussed the higher matters with Todros.

I argued: "If there is no God and if nature knows of no morality, why should man behave in a moral way? Why actually *shouldn't* he make pogroms?"

"And if—as you say—God is evil, why should man be good?" Todros countered my question with a question in Jewish fashion.

"To spite God," I replied. "Just because God wants men to kill each other and to slaughter innocent animals is why man must help man and animals, thus demonstrating that he doesn't approve of the way God runs the world."

"If God exists, don't you think He would have His way anyway? You think man is stronger than God?"

"No, I don't mean that at all. But man still has the right to protest if he considers God's deeds unjust."

"And how will this protest help?"

"It doesn't have to help. This is a form of statement that one opposes God's ways. If God kills and man kills, too, it means that we approve of the killing, and we can no longer blame God for the evils of the world."

I don't guarantee that these were my exact words, but this more or less was my contention. Todros shrugged. He was a humanist, a liberal, and an atheist, and he could conceive of no reason for reckoning with a God that didn't exist anyway. His approach was pragmatic. If you didn't kill others, others wouldn't kill you. Todros, incidentally, had been a pupil of my grandfather's. When Todros began to utter heretical remarks, Grandfather ordered him out of his house. My mother often spoke of Todros, and I had the feeling that as a young girl she had figured on becoming his wife. Mother was sixteen and a half when she married my father.

Another time, we got to talking about evil spirits. Todros, enlightened man that he was, naturally didn't believe in such things. I asked him if he recalled the incident of the spirit knocking on Avromele the slaughterer's window. The question apparently embarrassed Todros, for he began to stutter and shook his head.

After a while, he said: "I don't only remember it, I was there. We, the boys from the study house, went there every evening after the services."

"Did it really knock?"

"Yes, it did."

"A demon, eh?"

"I didn't say that."

"Who then did the knocking—a person?"

"I really don't know."

"Is it true that the *nachalnik* sent police and soldiers to see if someone was playing tricks?"

"I didn't see it, but it seems it was so. The whole town talked about it. Not only soldiers, other people searched around, too."

"Who was it that did the knocking?"

"I really don't know. There must have been some cause for it. One thing is sure—it wasn't a spirit because there are no such things."

I told Todros about my mother's dream, three days before the numbers were drawn, that Bashele, Mottel's wife, would win the lottery, and Todros said: "Yes, I remember that they spoke of this in your grandfather's house. It was nothing but a coincidence."

And Todros explained it to me this way—millions of dreams that made no sense or that predicted things that didn't happen were ignored. Among all those dreams it happened sometimes that one became true, and that was the one that was noticed. Many miracles could be explained away this way.

Several years went by. Poland had become independent again. My brother Joshua had come back from Russia with a wife and a child. I was straining to go back to Warsaw. I

was writing then, too, but neither my brother nor I was pleased with the results. My father had accepted a rabbinate in a small town in Galicia. I had gone to Warsaw a few times with the hope of getting some job there, but I came back each time after a few weeks to Bilgoraj. My brother had already written some of his best short stories by then, but he had no job either, and he lived in an alcove at his in-laws. Neither of us was good at any other kind of work, but to draw a living from Yiddish literature at that time was impossible. Literary Warsaw was dominated by the communists. A great number of the young writers and readers believed that communism would once and for all put an end to the Jewish problem. In a communist order there would be no Jews or gentiles, only a single united humanity. Religion and superstition would become a thing of the past. Neither my brother nor even less I fitted into this kind of ideology. I often spoke with great rage against God, but I had never ceased to believe in His existence. I wrote about spirits, demons, cabalists, dybbuks. Many Yiddish writers and readers had cut loose from their Jewish roots and from the juices upon which they had been nourished. They yearned once and for all to tear away from the ghetto and its culture—some as Zionists, others as radicals. Both factions preached worldliness. But I remained spiritually rooted deep in the Middle Ages (or so I was told). I evoked in my work memories and emotions that the worldly reader sought to forget and factually had forgotten. To the pious

Jews, on the other hand, I was a heretic and blasphemer. I saw to my astonishment that I belonged neither to my own people nor to any other peoples. Instead of fighting in my writings the political leaders of a decadent Europe and helping to build a new world, I waged a private war against the Almighty. From my viewpoint, the literature produced at that time in Soviet Russia, in Warsaw, and wherever the radicals held sway was fashioned to suit party resolutions rather than to express artistic truths. In the name of alleged progress, writers turned into liars and destroyed the little bit of talent God had bestowed upon them.

I lived on what I made by giving private lessons in Bilgoraj. Actually, I suffered extreme privation during those years, but I didn't take this to heart. I stopped reading the new literature and to the best of my ability read all the popular science books I could obtain as well as the magazines that described in everyday language what went on in the world of science. I speak here of the so-called exact sciences. I was less interested in works of psychology. Neither Freud, Adler, nor Jung seemed to touch on any truths that were previously unknown. I considered Bergson's *Creative Evolution* to be written with spirit and elegance, but with little else to offer. The astronomers had rejected the cosmology of Kant and Laplace, but as far as I could determine, they hadn't come up with a better theory. Each time I read an article about the origin of the universe, I

found that the author sooner or later came to the concept of a cosmic explosion that had erupted billions of years ago and made the universe flee from us with great rapidity. With each article I read, the universe grew larger, older, loaded with rays or particles that vibrated with fantastic frequency. Matter and energy had become one and the same. Those who studied the atom soon began to realize that the protons and electrons were insufficient to maintain the atom in balance. Long before neutrons were discovered, conjectures were made that the atom was more complicated than it had been assumed. Discoveries were made in chemistry and biology, too, but the mystery of the world and my own puzzlement grew no smaller. I myself was a collection of innumerable miracles—my skeleton, my flesh, my brain, my nerves. When I light a match, its light rays radiate at a speed of three hundred thousand kilometers a second. When I unwittingly step on a worm, I destroy a divine masterpiece. I myself was such a worm that could be squashed at any moment. I wanted to hope, but I had nothing to hope for. I wanted to resign, but I couldn't do that either. I read Tolstoi's sermons about Christian love and the nobility of the Russian peasant, but I knew that Tolstoi had never managed to acquire this Christian love himself and that the Russian muzhik wasn't so noble and honest as Tolstoi pictured him. His proposals that the land be divided among the peasants had come to naught. Millions of Russians starved to death; others had been sent to Siberia, rotted in prisons, or been stood against the wall by the GPU. I read the literary idols of the day—Romain Rolland, G. K. Chesterton, Thomas Mann. What I was searching for I could not find in their work.

8

In 1923 my brother Joshua became coeditor of the literary journal *Literary Pages,* and the mail brought me the news that I was given the post of proofreader. I had spent nine months in the half-bog, half-village where my father was rabbi. I had gone there because I had gotten sick in Bilgoraj. In this village there were no worldly books, and all I had with me were some old algebra textbooks and a copy of Spinoza's *Ethics.* I came to this village so broken in spirit that I was ready to give in to my parents, let them arrange a match for me (my love for Todros' daughter involved so many complications that I had to abandon all hopes), and become a storekeeper, a melamed, or whatever fate held in store for me. I stopped shaving my beard and let my earlocks grow. The inhabitants of the village were semi- or total peasants. Many Jews owned land in Galicia. I had no other company but my parents and my brother Moshe, who had become exceedingly pious during the time I had been away from home. The Jews there were all Belz Hasidim, but my brother had discovered that great Jewish mystic Rabbi Nachman Braclawer, and he became what was then called a Dead Hasid, which is to say, the disciple of a rabbi who no longer lived. I had heard of Rabbi Nachman

Braclawer while we were still living in Warsaw. I had read his wondrous tales years before I had glanced into his other works. My brother Moshe had obtained all of Rabbi Nachman's works, and since I had so much time on my hands, I began to read them. Rabbi Nachman was one of those blessed thinkers and poets whom—no matter how often you read or reread them—you always come away from with something new. As I've already mentioned, Rabbi Nachman didn't write these stories himself. He offered words of wisdom and told stories, and his pupil, Nathan the Nemirover, wrote them down. No one will ever know how much was lost in this process of transcription, but that which has remained is both great and deep. The famous Martin Buber discovered Rabbi Nachman Braclawer in his own fashion and translated his tales into German. Spirits such as Rabbi Nachman Braclawer cannot be forgotten. In each generation they are discovered anew.

Outside of his stories and maybe his prayers, Rabbi Nachman cannot be translated. His wisdom is closely bound up with passages in the Torah, in the Talmud. He ascribed to the Torah and the Gemara things that their writers never dreamed of. He often warped the meaning of their words, but what he had to say was always grand, fantastic, and full of deep psychological insight. I can firmly state that although Rabbi Nachman was a true saint, his spirit shouted a protest against the cruelties of life. To the best of his ability, he tried to justify the Almighty and to show that only good and mercy issued from Him, and that we ourselves were in great measure responsible for the sufferings that were visited upon us. At the same time he constantly wrestled with the dilemma of the good who suffered and the malefactor who enjoyed the best of everything. Like all great men, Rabbi Nachman was full of compassion. Each of his followers came to him with his own bag of troubles, and he had to comfort each one in turn while he himself was terribly ill and suffering unbearable pain. Rabbi Nachman died young, a victim of consumption.

I had lots of time in my father's town. I went through Spinoza's *Ethics* again and again. Out of Rabbi Nachman Braclawer's works screamed a kind of saintly hysteria, an exultation that often goes hand in hand with a deep melancholy, whereas Spinoza's *Ethics* was allegedly cold, pure logic. Spinoza didn't believe in feelings, in emotions, or, as he called them, affects. But it is obvious that beneath this cold logic lurks a person with a strong feeling for justice and truth. Just like Rabbi Nachman, Spinoza was a victim of consumption and died young. Both Rabbi Nachman and Spinoza suffered persecution. Other rabbis and their followers agitated against Rabbi Nachman for years. They even sought to excommunicate him. His worst enemy was a rabbi called the Spola Grandfather. In one of his better moments Rabbi Nachman said: "They've invented a person and they wrangle with him." The Jews of Holland actually excommunicated Spinoza. He was also in constant danger from the Inquisition, which was very powerful at that time. Rabbi Nachman found solace in a God who was full of benevolence and love, even though we humans could not comprehend His goodness. Spinoza found solace in a God who lacked will and feelings and possessed only great power and eternal laws. According to Spinoza, feelings, suffering, and justice were human concepts, passing modes.

I could find solace neither in Rabbi Nachman's God nor in Spinoza's. I had concluded that man had every right to protest against the violent acts of life. Man wasn't obliged to thank God for all the plagues and catastrophes that assailed him virtually from the cradle to the grave. The fact that God possessed immeasurably more knowledge and power than we did not give Him the right to torment us even if His motives were of the purest and wisest. The argument that the Lord presented to Job that He was wise and mighty while Job was a mere ignorant human was no answer to Job's anguish. Even the fact that toward the end of his life Job had more donkeys and camels and prettier daughters was little reward for his prior sufferings. I said to myself: I believe in God, I fear Him, yet I cannot love Him—not with my whole heart and soul as the Torah commands nor with the *amor Dei intellectualis* that Spinoza demands. Nor can I deny God as the materialists do. All I can do is to the best of my limits treat people and animals in

a way I consider proper. I had, one might say, created my own basis for an ethic—not a social ethic nor a religious one, but an ethic of protest. This ethic of protest, I told myself, existed in all people, in all animals, and in everything that lived and suffered. Even the evildoers protested when things started going badly for them and other malefactors did to them what they had done to others. As his diaries indicate, Napoleon, who sent millions of people to their deaths, protested bitterly on the island of St. Helena because he wasn't fed decently or tendered the proper respect. The moral person protests not only when he is personally wronged but also when he witnesses or thinks about the suffering of others. If God wants or feels compelled to torture His creatures, that is His affair. The true protester expresses his protest by avoiding doing evil to the best of his ability.

With this view of life and in this mood I went to Warsaw to become the proofreader of the *Literary Pages*.

Already on the train I had opportunity to witness the depths of human degradation, of Jewish anguish. A bunch of hooligans had boarded the third-class wagon that was filled with Jewish passengers—paupers traveling with sacks, bundles, and crates. The hooligans promptly turned their attention to these Jews. First they abused them with every kind of foul name. Every Jew, they insisted, was a Bolshevik, a Trotskyite, a Soviet spy, a Christ-killer, an exploiter. By the light of the tiny lamp hanging there I

could see these "exploiters"—ragged, broken people, most of whom were standing or squatting atop their belongings. The hooligans had earlier pushed the Jewish passengers off their seats and had sprawled themselves across the benches. One of them boasted that he had been an officer in the war. Several young Jewish men tried to defend the Jews and to point out that Jewish soldiers had fought at the front and suffered heavy casualties, but the hooligans hooted them down and heaped them with abuse. Soon, words turned into deeds. They grabbed the Jews' beards and yanked them. They tore the wig off an elderly Jewish woman. They began to stomp the Jews' belongings. The Jews could have easily beaten the hooligans to a pulp, but they knew how this would end. There were soldiers riding in the other cars, and it could have easily lead to bloodshed.

After a while the hooligans demanded that the Jews sing "Come, My Beloved," the hymn celebrating the coming of the Sabbath. It was a form of stigma and humiliation that many Polish hooligans had learned from the time when General Haller's soldiers had had their way with the Jews, had shaved off their beards often along with a piece of the cheek. I stood there frightened in a corner of the carriage near the toilet, gripping my bundle that consisted almost entirely of manuscripts and the few books that I possessed. Something inside me laughed at my own illusions. I knew full well that what I was seeing now was the essence of human history. Today the Poles tormented the Jews; yester-

day the Russians and Germans had tormented the Poles. Every history book was a tale of murder, torture, and injustice; every newspaper was drenched in blood and shame. The two most pessimistic philosophers I had read, Schopenhauer and Von Hartmann, both condemned suicide, but at that moment I knew that there was only one true protest against the horror of life and that was to hurl back to God His gift. It was entirely possible that had I had a pistol or poison with me at that time, I would have killed myself.

After much talk and pleading, the Jews began to sing "Come, My Beloved." It was a half-song, half-lament. Until that night I had often fantasized about redeeming the human species, but it became obvious to me then that the human species didn't deserve redemption. To do so would actually be a crime. Man was a beast that killed, ravaged, and tortured not only other species but its own as well. The other's pain was his joy, the other's humiliation his glory. The Torah tells us that God regretted having created man. Adam's son murdered his brother. Ten generations later, God caused the Flood because the world had grown corrupt. There isn't a book that so candidly and clearly tells the truth about man and his nature than the Scriptures. Even the allegedly good people are evil. Yesterday's martyrs often become today's bullies. Man, as a species, deserves all the whippings he gets. It is not mere chance that most of the monuments man is erecting are to murderers—be it patriotic murderers or revolutionary murderers. In Russia there is even a monument to Bogdan Chmielnicki. The real innocent martyrs on this earth are the animals, particularly the herbivorous.

After a while the hooligans grew tired, leaned their heads against the backs of the seats, and began to snore. The little storekeepers in this car were obviously innocent, but I knew for a fact that Jewish youths in Russia also tortured and killed innocent people in the name of the Revolution, often their own Jewish brothers. The Jewish communists in Bilgoraj predicted that when the revolution came, they would hang my uncle Joseph and my uncle Itche for being clergymen, Todros the watchmaker for being a bourgeois, my friend Notte Schwerdscharf for being a Zionist, and me for daring to doubt Karl Marx. They also promised to root out the Bundists, the Poale Zionists, and, naturally, the pious Jews, the Orthodox. For these small-town youths it had been enough to read a few brochures to turn them into potential butchers. Some of them even said that they would execute their own parents. A number of these youths perished years later in Stalin's slave camps.

9

The new Polish republic was barely four years old, but in that brief time it had already gone through a war with the Bolsheviks, party struggles that led to an assassination of a President, attacks upon Jews in a number of towns, bitter disputes with the Ruthenians who had become part of the new Poland, and a rising inflation. Lenin still lived, but he was already paralyzed, and Comrade Stalin was beginning to make a name for himself. In Germany a former paper hanger named Hitler had launched an abortive *Putsch*. In Italy Mussolini forced castor oil down his opponents' throats. The typhus epidemics and hungers had decimated who knows how many people, but the streets of Warsaw still swarmed with pedestrians and you couldn't get an apartment. All cellars, all garrets, were jammed with tenants and subtenants. From all the provinces people tore to come to Warsaw, but there was no work to be had there. Even as the Polish Socialist party trumpeted that the proletariat of all nations must unite, its professional unions barred Jewish workers. Actually there wasn't even enough work for the gentile workers. The Bundists, the Jewish socialists, sharply criticized their Christian comrades for their nationalistic and capitalistic

deviations from Karl Marx's teachings. The Warsaw communists, Jews nearly all, heaped brimstone and fire upon all the parties and insisted that only in Soviet Russia did true social justice prevail. The Zionists argued that there was no longer any hope for Jews in the lands of the Diaspora. Only in Palestine would the Jew be able to live freely and develop. But England held the mandate and wouldn't allow any Jewish immigration. The Arabs had already begun to threaten the Jews with pogroms.

From my very first day in Warsaw I had no place to stay, since my brother lived with his wife and child in a tiny room at his in-laws and in the direst poverty. Melech Ravich, one of the editors of the *Literary Pages,* took me into his apartment for free, an apartment which consisted of several attic rooms on the fifth floor. Just as I was a skeptic, so was Ravich—and is to this day—a believer. He believed in the redeeming power of literature, in socialism, in humanism, in the philosophy of Spinoza. At that time I wasn't yet a vegetarian. How could someone who had nothing to eat be a vegetarian? But Melech Ravich was already a vegetarian. He was tall, stout, eleven years older than I, and handsome. I actually could speak nothing but Yiddish, even though I could read several languages. But Melech Ravich spoke good Polish and German. He had spent years in Vienna working in a bank. His wife had a good voice and aspired to a singing career. Outside of my brother, Melech Ravich was my first contact with the literary world and with the so-called big world. We began our discussions immediately. Ravich believed with absolute faith that the world of justice could come today or tomorrow. All men would become brothers and sooner or later, vegetarians, too. There would be no Jews, no gentiles, only a single united mankind whose goal would be equality and progress. Literature, Ravich felt, could help hasten this joyous epoch. I respected his talent and his worldly knowledge, yet at the same time I wondered at his naïveté. All the omens pointed to the fact that the human species had learned nothing from the war that had cost twenty million lives, if not more. In all the cities of Europe people did the latest dances—the Charleston, the fox trot, or whatever they were called—dances over graves. Sociologists propounded theories that were allegedly new, but they exuded the evils of generations. Poets babbled their empty verses. The *Literary Pages,* of which I was proofreader, was radical, socialistic, half communistic, full of bad articles, poor poems, and false criticism. My brother soon turned away from the editorship. The one who had top say there were Nachman Maisel, who had for years flitted between socialism and communism before becoming a full-fledged communist, and Peretz Markish, who sang odes to Stalin until Stalin had him liquidated. Peretz Markish and Melech Ravich were also the editors of an anthology called *The Gang,* which flattered the rabble and catered to its basest instincts. It cast aspersions upon Jewishness and Jewish history; it denigrated

the classicists of world literature, and as an example of the new literature, it featured the hollow phrases of Mayakovsky. Although I was young and far from being a mature writer, I wasn't fooled by all these lies and flatteries. Behind this gabble lurked the urge to destroy, the will for a new mass violence. Malthus' God wasn't yet sated. The emissaries of Moscow called for a world pogrom upon all the bourgeois and middle classes as well as upon all socialists who dared deviate from Lenin by even a hair. Provincial youths—yesterday's Yeshiva students who never in their lives had done a lick of work nor had been able to do so— spoke in the name of the workers and peasants and condemned to death all those who wouldn't stand on their side of the barricade. I looked on with alarm and astonishment at how a few pamphlets could transform into potential murderers the sons and daughters of a race that hadn't held a sword in hand for two thousand years. It had become the fashion among the girls to wear the leather jackets worn in Russia by the female members of the Cheka. The mothers and fathers of these murderers were scheduled to become their first victims. . . .

Spinoza had warned me against the emotions, affects that darkened reason and actually constituted a form of madness. In the books of morals I had scanned during the nine months I had spent in my parents' town, these same emotions were called evil thoughts, the persuasions of

Satan. Rabbi Nachman Braclawer, a man in whom the emotions seethed and stewed, offered all kinds of advice on how to outwit and master them. Man was a pauper when it came to reason, but a millionaire when it came to emotions. I myself was a ferment of passions and doubts. Dreams assailed me like locust. My nights were filled with nightmares. I hadn't yet been with a woman, but in my imagination I had already committed all the excesses that could only be fancied. I wanted to write and to study, but 90 per cent of my spiritual energy was squandered on yearning for the forbidden, that which would be harmful to me and to others. Like all tyrants of all times, I wanted to force my ideas upon others. I flew to the farthest galaxies with a speed a hundred or a thousand times faster than light. I discovered such potions that granted me Divine wisdom. Like the legendary Joseph de la Rinah, about whom I had read as a boy, I lured all the beauties of the world to my bed through magic. The summer had passed and it started to turn cold. I couldn't stay on forever in Melech Ravich's congested apartment, and I started to look for a room of my own. I suffered hunger, cold, sickness. The financial situation of the *Literary Pages* was such that they couldn't even pay me the few groschen I had been promised. In my despair I allowed many errors to go by and stood to lose even this miserable job. My brother's lot was no better than mine. In the midst of all my grandiose daydreams, a voice

within me cried: "Put an end to it! You have nothing to wait for. With a rope or a razor you can free yourself of all this misery. There is but one redemption and that is death."

That winter in Warsaw there were two institutions that kept me alive. One was the Writers' Club, where I was allowed to come as a guest. It was warm there, one could read the Yiddish and Hebrew newspapers from all over the world or play chess, and the food at the buffet counter was reasonable. Occasionally, the waitresses even extended credit. Every few evenings a lecture was held, and I met many young writers—beginners like myself in the same dire straits as I. They all strove to have something published in the *Literary Pages*, and they may have assumed that I had some influence there. They heaped scorn on the established writers whose poems, stories, and articles I corrected. I realized something then that I had actually already known for a long time—that poor writers are often astute critics of other writers. Their criticism was sharp and accurate. Some even correctly pinpointed the errors of the great writers. But this didn't stop them from writing with a clumsiness that astounded me. The same held true in the way they appraised the character of others. Egotists spoke with contempt of egotists, fools derided the stupidity of fools, boors demonstrated refinement in pointing out other men's boorishness, exploitative traits, vanity. A mysterious chasm loomed between their estimation of others and of themselves. It seemed that somewhere within, each person was able to see the truth if only he was determined not to overlook it. Self-love was apparently the strongest hypnotic force, just as it is written in the Pentateuch: "For the gift blindeth the wise, and perverteth the words of the righteous." The sage becomes blind and the saint will compromise with the evildoer when it suits his purpose, or when he *thinks* that it suits his purpose.

The other institution that sustained me was the libraries. For years I had suffered a hunger for books. In Warsaw I could get all the books I wanted. I went to the same Bresler's Library and spent hours browsing there. There was a table where you could sit and read. I read and scanned through books on philosophy, psychology, biology, astronomy, physics. I went to the municipal library on Koszykowa Street and read scientific journals.

I didn't understand everything I read, but I didn't have to. Science offered me scant comfort. The stars were composed of the same matter as earth—hydrogen, oxygen, iron, copper, sulfur. They radiated vast amounts of energy that were lost in space or maybe transformed into matter again. From time to time a star exploded and became a nova. Enormous clouds of dust floated in space in the process of becoming stars billions of years hence. As far as the astronomers could tell, there was no life on the other planets of our solar system. As for probing the possibilities of life beyond the solar system, there was no hope for that. Neither Einstein's theory nor any other theories held out any promise for the species of man. We already had radio sets in Poland, and when you put on the earphones you might hear jokes from vaudeville, a report on the political situation, or possibly even an anti-Semitic speech. Writers predicted television and airplanes that would cross the Atlantic, but these predictions did nothing to elevate my spirit. . . .

Once as I browsed in Bresler's Library, I came across a complete translation or an abridgment of Edmund Gurney, Frederick W. H. Myers, and Frank Podmore's *Phantasms of the Living.* I took to this work with an eagerness that astounded even me. If even a hundredth part of the cases described there was true, all values would have to be reassessed. The writers were men who hadn't the slightest reason to lie or falsify. Almost all the incidents had been thoroughly investigated. I learned of the English Society for Psychical Research. Even here in Poland such investigations were being conducted. Each day brought me some fresh news. The French astronomer Camille Flammarion had investigated hundreds of cases of mind reading, clairvoyance, true dreams and had written works about this that had been translated into Polish or German. Poland had a Professor Ochorowicz and a world-famous medium, Kluski. The Italian scholar Cesare Lombroso, who had been a materialist all his life, in his old age had become a spiritualist and participated in séances. I got the opportunity to read the works, or fragments of works, of Sir Oliver Lodge,

Sir William Crookes, Sir Arthur Conan Doyle—the creator of Sherlock Holmes, which I had read as a boy in Yiddish translation and which had so enthralled me. In the science taught at the universities, man was ashes and dust. He lived out his few years and became lost forever. But the psychical researchers stated directly or indirectly that the body contained a soul. The twenty million people who had perished in the war were somewhere about. I read cases of dogs, cats, and parrots coming back to their owners after death and giving signs of their love and devotion.

I was inclined to believe that which I read without further guarantees, but I recalled what I had told myself only two weeks earlier—that self-love and self-interest were a colossal hypnotic force. I had read a translation of William James's *The Will to Believe*. Every kind of fantasy nourished itself upon this will. The fact that official science offered me no comfort was no proof that it lied. As much as I yearned to believe the psychical researchers, I realized full well that all their contentions were based on what this or the other person had related to them. I also got hold of books by writers who denied all the assertions of spiritualists and psychical researchers. Even at that time they had already unearthed many swindlers among the mediums. I didn't dare let myself be bribed by my own desires! I had to personally investigate and reassure myself that I wasn't paying myself off to close my eyes to the truth.

I became so deeply engrossed in these matters that I forgot all my troubles. I read books about psychical research well into the night until my eyes closed. In the morning I rose with renewed curiosity. I had rented a room that was unheated and had bedbugs to boot. My clothes had grown tattered, nor did I get enough to eat, but I didn't let these petty annoyances get me down. I no longer played chess at the Writers' Club nor waged debates about literature. I took along books and read them at the club. The writers made fun of me. To this day elderly writers from Warsaw remind me of how I sat at the club reading books. The writers used to glance at the titles of these books and shrug. In the Yiddishist circles they virtually didn't know that such reading matter even existed.

The winter passed—I rightly didn't know how—and spring came. My room was no longer so cold. At this time I met a man and a woman who came to influence my life.

10

Even before coming to Warsaw I had heard of Hillel and
Aaron Zeitlin. Two giants—father and son—had evolved
in Yiddish literature in the radical, atheistic atmosphere of
a Jewish culture that was ignorant and provincial besides.
The father, Hillel Zeitlin, who was learned in philosophy
and a cabalist, had come to the early conclusion that a
modern Jewishness (whether in nationalistic or socialistic
form) that lacked religion was a paradox and an absurdity.
Hillel Zeitlin lived in a milieu that dictated worldly Jewishness. Bialik the Hebraist and Peretz the Yiddishist both
maintained that the Jews could be a people even without
religion. Bialik contended that this could be possible only
in a Jewish nation, whereas Peretz advocated that Jews
should fight for national autonomy in the lands where
they lived. But Hillel Zeitlin postulated powerful arguments that Jewishness without religion—a Jewishness
based on a language or even upon a nation—lacked the
force to keep the Jews united. What's more, such Jews
wouldn't be Jews but gentiles who happened to speak
Yiddish or Hebrew. Even prior to Zeitlin, Ahad Ha-am had
offered similar opinions, but Ahad Ha-am had himself been
an agnostic, a doubter of the religious truths, one for whom

religion had been merely a means of keeping the Jews together. It's needless to say that such a religiousness would hold no appeal for anyone. On the other hand, Hillel Zeitlin was a deeply religious man whose religious convictions mounted with the years. Hillel Zeitlin was a genuine mystic, a man who perceived the vanity of vanities that made up the world as well as its contradictions and illusions. He bore within him the religious fervor of the Jews of yore. It's a fact that the extreme Orthodox didn't look up to him. To them, he was a heretic. Hillel Zeitlin had studied philosophy and had published a book in Yiddish, *The Problems of Good and Evil.* I found more philosophy in this book than in all the other books of this kind put together. He didn't quibble over details but went straight to the essence of things. Even the ice-cold philosophers turned hot in the glow of his light. His son, Aaron Zeitlin, was a great religious poet, in my opinion one of the greatest in world literature. Like his father, he was a mystic and a cabalist; he actually formulated his own concept of the cabala. I had read his poems while still in Bilgoraj and had grown enchanted by them. In his early years his style was a bit too muddled and "modernistic," but later on he realized that one can be both deep *and* clear. Although Aaron Zeitlin had received a modern education and knew languages and world literature, he remained essentially a Yeshiva student, a bookish man and an intellectual in the truest sense of the word. We became acquainted at the Writers' Club.

There was a windowless room there where the lights were always on, one wall always stayed warm. It was connected to the oven of a restaurant that was kept constantly heated. In winter I often sat by this wall and read. I apparently suffered from low blood pressure, since I often felt cold even in the summer. The Gemara has a word for it: "A donkey stays cold even in the month of Tammuz."

One day in spring as we both stood by this wall warming ourselves, we struck up an acquaintance which soon turned into a friendship that was to last a lifetime. Zeitlin was some six or seven years older than I and by then already a well-known, mature poet and essayist, and I was an unknown beginner. It's obvious why I should have been eager to know him, but I can't understand to this day why he should have taken an interest in me. We were very much different in character, and this difference intensified over the years. I saw his faults clearly, as he did mine. I liked women; from the very first I wrote about sex in such a way as to shock the Yiddish critics and often the readers, too; he was decidedly monogamous and a romantic. Books were only a part of my life, but to Zeitlin a book was virtually life itself. As restrained as he was in his own behavior, so wise was he to all the human passions. I waged a private war with the Almighty, but Zeitlin always defended Him. He might have easily been a recluse or a monk. We disagreed occasionally, but we remained friends.

The Yiddish writers who for years were nearly to a man

infected with leftism castigated the Zeitlins, both the father and the son. When I grew older and they read my writings, it sent them into a rage. Neither Aaron Zeitlin nor I fitted into Yiddish literature with its sentimentality and clichés about social justice or Jewish nationalism. Both Zeitlin and I were deeply interested in psychic research. We both (actually all three—the elder Zeitlin, too) realized that the writers whom the Yiddish and Hebrew critics considered major figures and classicists were in fact often inept provincials. It didn't take us long to realize that what prevailed in Yiddish literature held true in all the world literatures, too. Every true talent was an oasis in a desert of tastelessness. When he is still young, he assumes that he can push back the sands and transform the desert into a paradise, but as he grows older, he realizes that he should thank God that the desert didn't swallow him up the way it already had many others. What's more, since God had created the desert, the desert had every reason to exist. Where did it say that green grass was more important or even prettier than brown sand? . . .

We often sat for hours then—and years later, too—conversing. We both believed in God, in demons, evil spirits, in all kinds of ghosts and phantoms. In those days Aaron Zeitlin was deeply concerned that the Yiddish critics cut him to pieces, and he often railed against them bitterly. I observed with shame that when a critic occasionally did praise him, Zeitlin changed his opinion of the critic virtually on the spot. This, as far as I know, was Zeitlin's only fault. I had many other, bigger faults, but I couldn't tolerate this particular weakness in Zeitlin, even though he made no mention of *my* shortcomings.

That spring I also met a woman who in her own fashion was a mystic, too, and who came to influence my life and my writing. By then I had already had some doings with women—but always in a hurry and in an atmosphere of fear. I might say that I snatched a taste of love here and there which inevitably left me unfulfilled, confused, and occasionally ashamed as well. Older people often said they envied my youth, but I knew that there was nothing to envy. A day didn't go by that I didn't contemplate suicide. My biggest torment was my lack of success in my writing. I would write something that seemed to me good, but I soon picked it apart and tore it to pieces. I searched about for a criterion by which to judge literature, but I couldn't find it. I frequently awoke filled with doubt and went to bed in the same state of mind. I often had the feeling that someone had bewitched me. I wanted to write one thing, but what emerged was something else altogether. I formulated a plan for a story, but the plan slipped through my fingers.

Spring had come and balmy breezes blew outside. I had to find another place, since the people from whom I subleased wanted the room for themselves. I spent weeks looking for a place, but the rents were too high all over and the rooms seemed cold, damp, insufficiently lighted. My

feet hurt from climbing endless flights of stairs. I might have laid the whole burden on my brother's shoulders, but it's not in me to whine. Besides, my brother had problems of his own.

On that particular day I didn't go looking for a room. I got up late and went to the Writers' Club. On the way there I bought a bagel, and I ate it right in the street. The sun was shining, but I felt cold and shivered. I sat down by the warm wall and began to read some book on hypnotism, occultism, magnetism, or however the author described the hidden powers. It told of a man over whom his dead mother had been keeping watch for many years. Each time he faced danger he heard her voice warning him. She gave him advice, even brought him together with the woman he married. The man told this story himself and provided names and addresses of witnesses who corroborated everything he said. If this story was true, I told myself, it behooved me to lead a different kind of life. I had to dedicate myself to disseminating these truths, to convincing mankind that there was no such thing as death. That being the case, it made no sense whatsoever to commit suicide. . . .

Someone came over and tapped me on the shoulder—it was one of the young poets.

He said: "You still read this nonsense?"

"Do me a favor and read just this page!"

He took the book and glanced at it.

"Old wives' tales, hallucinations, crap! Opium to lull the masses!"

We talked awhile, and he said: "Are you still looking for a room?"

"Yes, very much so."

"I know of a woman who wants to give up a room. She's a distant relative of mine, a granddaughter of rabbis. If the room isn't rented yet, you'll fall into paradise. She's one of your kind, a bit touched. She sits at a tilting table all night and tries to look into the future. Her father was a rabbi who went off his head. She tries to write, to paint. She's gone through three husbands already."

"How old is she?"

"She could be your mother, but she likes young fellows. Wait, it seems I've jotted down her address somewhere."

He took out a notebook which was filled with addresses and with poems inscribed in tiny letters. He found the address and gave it to me.

I asked whether the woman had a telephone, and he replied: "She used to, but it's been shut off. She would have been evicted, too, but the landlord is a Hasid of her uncle."

The woman lived somewhere on Gesia Street near the Jewish cemetery. "I won't get involved with her," I promptly resolved. I abhorred dissolute females. I longed for a woman who would be pure and chaste and would

learn about love only from me. Still, I headed straight for
Gesia Street. The closer I came to the house, the more
funerals I saw—one hearse after another, some followed
by weeping women, others without mourners. Here I was
looking for a room, but these people had already finished
living, hoping, and suffering and were being transported
to eternity. The horses took step after deliberate step. They
were draped in black cloths with holes cut out for eyes,
and these holes were filled with pupil. I imagined that
those horses knew what they were transporting and that
they were making an accounting of their own souls. If the
cabalists were right that everything is godliness, the horses
were part of God, too. . . .

I entered a courtyard with peeling walls and a huge garbage bin in the center much like on Krochmalna Street
where my family used to live. A huckster with a sack over
his shoulders cried: "I buy clo'! I buy clo'! I buy clo'!" and
cast his eyes upward toward the topmost windows. The sun
stood fixed in the center of the sky and poured gold down
upon the cobblestones, the gutters, the raggedy children,
the huckster's reddish beard. A spring breeze blew carrying
the smells of blossoms and the manure used to fertilize the
fields. I even thought that I detected the stench of the
corpses. I climbed three flights and came to rest before a
door that thirty years ago might have been red but was now
a faded brown. The door handle dangled listlessly; the
number on the door was half off. I knocked, but no one an-

swered. "I knew that I was wasting my time," I told myself. I was filled with envy for the dead, who were provided with perpetual quarters and with everything else a corpse didn't need. . . . I knocked again and again. I was too exhausted to go on looking for rooms. Suddenly I heard a woman's voice behind me. I looked backward and saw the lady of the house. She appeared to be in her late thirties or possibly forty. Although it was a weekday, she wore a silk cape and a black dress that wasn't fashionably short but hung almost to the ankles. Over her red hair—also unstylishly long and combed into a chignon—sat a black silk hat, the kind that was worn forty years prior. Her face was white, her eyes a blend of green and yellow. One glance sufficed to note that she had once been a beauty. In one hand she carried a purse, in the other a basket of groceries. She had apparently just been shopping.

"May I know, young man, whom you're looking for?"

I took out the piece of paper on which the young poet had scribbled her name and address and said: "Mrs. Gina Halbstark."

"I am Gina Halbstark."

The woman (I'm not giving her right name here) stopped, and we confronted each other. She appeared both girlish and prematurely aged, like someone who has just gotten up from an illness. Her cheeks were sunken, her chin was narrow, her nose thin, her neck long, her red hair faded. Earrings were dangling from her lobes. For all her fancy dress there was a kind of genteel seediness about her. Her eyes reflected curiosity as well as a familial intimacy as if by some mysterious instinct she would have known who I was and why I had come. I moved aside, and she unlocked the door and led me into a corridor and from there into a big room. The apartment exuded the same genteel air of neglect as its owner. She asked me to sit down and opened the door to a tiny cubicle, an alcove with apparently no windows, since it was dark in there. She went off and tarried a long time, then came back wearing a house coat, her hair combed and her face powdered—all this before I even told her the reason for my visit. I asked her if she had a room to rent, and she said: "Yes, but only for a bat who doesn't need light."

"I'm a bat," I said.

"You don't look it," she countered, "but you can never tell what a person is."

We began to talk, and literally within minutes there evolved between us a kind of intimacy that astounded me. One moment we were strangers and the next we were chatting away as if we had been friends for years. She recounted her genealogy to me, and I learned all about her grandfathers and great-grandfathers, the books they had written, their honorable lives and piety. She told me who her first husband had been—I had heard of his father. She herself had grown "corrupt" early in life and had turned to worldly Yiddish and enlightened Hebrew books by such authors as Isaac Joel Linetzki, Mendele Mocher Sforim, Abraham Mapu, Shalom Aleichem, Peretz, as well as Yiddish translations of Tolstoi, Dostoevski, Lermontov, Knut Hamsun, Strindberg, and such Polish writers as Mickiewicz, Slowacki, Wyspianski, and Przybyszewski. Not only had I read exactly the same books but I was thoroughly familiar with their appearance, the number of pages they contained, and who their publishers and translators were.

Gina Halbstark had read my brother's works, and she even knew about me. I asked her how this could be, and she retorted: "Warsaw is a small town."

As if of its own volition the conversation drifted to the occult powers, and when Gina heard that I was interested in such things, her face grew animated and youthful. In that very dark room that she was trying to rent she kept a whole library of books and magazines devoted to these topics. She took me into the room and switched on the light. I saw a caseful of books on theosophy, spiritualism, hypnotism, and animal magnetism, in Polish, German, and French, and stacks of magazines.

I asked her how much the rent would be, and she said: "You'll pay whatever you can afford."

And she smiled with rabbinical amiability and said that she would prepare lunch for me.

"What have I done to deserve this?" I asked, and she replied: "Because I like you."

I followed her out, and in the corridor I embraced her and we began to kiss with the fervor of reunited lovers. She kissed and bit me. "I know you from an earlier life. . . ."

11

God in heaven—what a great stroke of luck had befallen me! I had been prepared to throw back to God His gift in a rage, but I was obviously destined to still live, suffer, to wrong myself and others. I sprawled now on the very same bed where I had lain with Gina, and I slept, probably like Esau did after he sold his birthright for a mess of pottage. In my dreams I was in Warsaw, in Bilgoraj, and in the town where my father was rabbi. Gina and Todros the watchmaker's daughter merged into one and at the same time became my mother and my sister Hindele. "What's happening to me?" I exclaimed in my sleep. "I'm losing the world to come!"

Someone within me—my father? my grandfather? a head of a Yeshiva?—conducted a sermon and admonished me: "You've desecrated your soul. You are defiled! You've copulated with Lilith, Naamah, Machlat, Shibta! . . ."

This dream was a continuation of the reality. In bed with me Gina spoke like both a holy woman and a whore. She screamed so loud I was afraid the neighbors would come running. She sang, wept, quoted passages from the Song of Songs, called herself Rahab the harlot. It was she who had saved the spies that Joshua son of Nun had sent out to spy on Jericho, and they had lain in her arms. I, Itchele, was one of them. In other reincarnations I was Abraham and she Hagar, I Reuben and she Bilhah, I Boaz and she Ruth, I David and she Bath-sheba. . . . She whispered secrets and licked my ear. She promptly began to instruct me in new positions, variations, and in her own mad caprices. I questioned her about her former husbands and lovers, and she bellowed: "I long for them all! I'd like to have them all at the same time so that they would tear me to pieces and leave nothing of me to bury! They should spit upon me and drown me in their saliva. . . ."

I had read Forel and maybe Krafft-Ebing, too, and I already knew about sadism, masochism, fetishism, and a number of other such *isms,* but all that which was paper and ink there turned here into throbbing life, savage lust, a singing and lamenting madness. She roused both desire and revulsion within me. We had spent a spring day in a wakeful nightmare and now the dream added its own absurdities.

I opened my eyes, and it was dark not only here but in the other room, too. Instead of making lunch for me, Gina prepared dinner. The smells of meat, potatoes, onion, garlic, carried from the kitchen. She sang there and poured water into sizzling stew. I had awakened thirsty, hungry, tired, yet eager for new larks and adventures. "Am I happy?" I asked myself, and someone within me replied:

"No." "Why not?" I countered, but the other remained silent. I cocked my ears and listened to myself. My ideal had always been a decent Jewish daughter, not some whore who had wallowed in every slime. I partly loved this Gina, partly hated her. The preacher from my dream seized upon this and argued: "It's because of such abominations that the whole human race suffers. The Canaanites and Amalekites committed such outrages. It was her kind that caused the damnation of cities. Wars and violence stem from adultery. It was her kind that gave themselves over to the enemies of Israel, and it was their children who made pogroms upon the Jews. . . ."

My head fell back against the pillow, and I lay there in mute bewilderment. I had promised my father that I would conduct myself as a Jew in Warsaw. On the way here I had even related my philosophy of protest to Jewishness. The Jew personified the protest against the injustices of nature and even those of the Creator. Nature wanted death, but the Jew opted for life; nature wanted licentiousness, but the Jew asked for restraint; nature wanted war, but the Jew, particularly the Diaspora Jew (the highly developed Jew), sought peace. The Ten Commandments were in themselves a protest against the laws of nature. The Jew had taken upon himself the mission of vanquishing nature and of harnessing it in such a way that it served the Ten Commandments. Because the Jew went against nature, it despised him and took revenge upon him. But the victory lay on the side of the Jew. Even if he had to wage war against God, the Jew would not desist. According to the Talmud, even a voice from heaven should be ignored if it is not on the side of justice. When the Jew knew that something was right, he dared oppose the Almighty Himself. . . .

These had been my thoughts on the train when the hooligans ordered the Jews to sing "Come, My Beloved." At that time the faces of the Jews had shown a resoluteness that was not of this world. Well, but this kind of strength lay only within the Jew who observed the Torah, not in the modern Jew who served nature like the gentile, was subservient to it, and placed all his hopes upon it. . . .

I heard footsteps. Gina stood in the doorway.

"Are you asleep?"

"No."

"You dozed off like an infant at my breast. Are you hungry?"

"No. Yes."

"Come eat. Come, I need you. You are my last hope. I was ready to die already, but suddenly you came and—"

She switched on the light, but I asked her to put it out again. I was ashamed before her. She had put on a costly robe, but I had nothing besides the clothes I had come in. In the course of the single day my cheeks had sprouted a sharp stubble. Gina went back to the kitchen while I fumbled with my garments and shoes in the dark.

Later when we were eating, Gina confided that she had

anticipated my arrival and had actually been waiting for me. She practiced automatic writing, and one night her hand had written my name perhaps a hundred times. She often posed questions to a table with wooden pegs and to a Ouija board, and they both concurred that her great and last lover would be as red-haired as she was. She told me that she knew some other things about me which she couldn't reveal to me as yet. She tipped her head to the side and studied me sidelong with female expertise and not without mockery, as if she would have played a trick on me which would become apparent to me later. I felt ashamed of myself in view of her sexual experience, and I thought of the many men she had had before me.

She seemed to guess my thoughts because she said: "You've wiped them all away. From now on, you're my whole life."

We drank tea, and stories poured from Gina's lips. She had caught typhus during the war and been taken to a hospital where the doctors tried to poison her. She wouldn't be alive now but for her dead grandmother who came to her in a dream and warned her not to take the medicine. This same grandmother had saved her from death several other times. Once when she lay all alone in the house ill with influenza and without any food (it was after her second divorce), this same grandmother brought her a glass of warm milk.

Gina stood up and solemnly vowed that she was speaking the truth. The glass on her night table had been empty. Suddenly, it had filled with milk, and she had heard her grandmother's voice: "Drink!" As soon as she drank the milk, her fever subsided and she recovered.

"Believe me or don't—what does it matter to me what you believe? You won't give me your millions in any case, but I swear on my dead mother and father, may they rest in peace, that I'm not lying to you. If I'm lying, may I not live to—"

"I believe you, I believe you, but it could have been a hallucination that came from the fever."

"I knew that's what you would say. It was no hallucination. My temperature was only 98.6°. Even when it rises above 104°, I remain fully conscious. I once had an operation for my appendix, and the doctor couldn't put me to sleep with the chloroform no matter how he tried. He gave me the biggest possible dose, and still I remained conscious. I felt the pains when they cut into me, and I heard every word he said to the nurses. Incidentally, in the middle of the operation I suddenly began to fly in the air. I glanced down and saw my body, the surgeon, the nurses, and all the rest. This was the first time I went into the astral plane and you can imagine my terror when I saw my own body lying there. I was sure that I was dead. All of a sudden something trembled within me, and I re-entered my body and felt the pains anew. The doctor told me later that my heart had stopped for a while and he had thought I was done for.

Why am I telling you all this? Yes, to prove that I don't lose consciousness so easily. I sleep and at the same time I hear every rustle and think wakeful thoughts. I didn't have even a lick of milk in the house at that time. I had nothing at all. Suddenly a glass of milk stood there before me. When I drank it, it tasted as if it had come fresh from the udder. Each sip brought a surge of strength with it. I also heard my grandmother's voice as clearly as I hear you now. What do you say to this, eh?"

"If the dead live and can milk a cow in a hurry and bring a glass of milk through a closed door, then our whole science isn't worth a fig. In that case—"

"Yes, they do live and they can do many things. Not all the souls remain below—most of them go off to other worlds. But my grandmother was terribly close to me, and she didn't want to be parted from me. She knew my accursed nature and crazy ways and how easy it was for me to risk my life. If not for her I wouldn't be here now. Don't laugh, but my grandmother even told me about you. One time she spent half the night with me. I said: 'Grandma, I don't want to live anymore. I've had enough of the disappointments, of men's falsehood and all the rest. So long as there is another world,' I said, ' a prettier world without evil and boorishness and all the unhappiness and complications. I'd rather be there. I want to be with you, Grandma,' I said. I'm not a crier by nature, but I began to weep furiously, and she said: 'Genendele'—that's what she called me

—'it's not our world but God's, and everyone who is sent there has some mission and a time in which to perform it. Your time to leave hasn't come yet. Some good still awaits you.' 'What is it?' I asked. 'Another man?' And she said, 'He is still a child, but he is also a man and he will be your final comfort.' She said something else, but I don't want to tell you what. First you spoke like a believer, and all of a sudden you become a skeptic and look at me as if I were crazy."

"I believe in God, but there are things that are awfully hard to accept."

"Eh? If you will stay with me, you'll see things with your own eyes so that you'll be spared having to believe in them. I was resolved not to tell you what my grandmother said about us—it seems she even warned me against talking to you about her, but she is used to it now that I disobey her. I wish I *had* listened to her—I would have spared myself lots of heartache."

"What did she say about us?"

"She said that we would collaborate on a book."

"What kind of book?"

"I don't know. She didn't give me any details. I want you to know that she has never yet told me anything that hasn't come true. Sometimes immediately, other times years later. But the last time she spoke to me I did begin to feel something like doubt. I had taken a holy vow to have nothing further to do with any other man and certainly not with one younger than I. I had also given up my writing. Whatever I wrote the editors sent back. They often sent back things they hadn't even bothered to read. This, as the saying goes, is a chapter in itself. I have countless enemies. They hate me, first of all because God cursed me with talent, and secondly because they know that I'm wise to all their filthy tricks and intrigues and that I can't be so easily fooled. It's enough for me to glance at a person to know all his secrets. Believe me this is no idle boast. Nor is it a favorable trait either. Actually, it's a tragedy. God capped the brain with a skull so that others shouldn't see what goes on inside it. How can you live knowing what someone else is thinking? Thirdly, they hate me because I come from the finest stock while they are all boors from the very dregs. Why am I telling you all this, eh? Yes, they hate me. They would drown me in a spoonful of warm water, as the saying goes. Therefore, since there was no longer any hope of love or literature for me, what sense did it make for me to go on living? But since my grandmother said that we must write a book together, we will write a book whether you want to or not."

"How do you go about writing a book together?"

"Eh? I don't know myself. You'll write a page and I'll write a page and between pages we'll kiss. How would you like that?"

"Very much so!"

"Well, you're still completely a child. You're like a

young horse with a growing passion who plays up to his own mother. But you mustn't have any bad memories of me."

"What makes you say that?"

"Oh, I won't be around much longer. Eat all your dessert, don't leave anything over."

12

I soon noted that Gina was obsessed with death. We lay in bed, and she spoke of buying a plot together at the Gesia Street cemetery. I had to promise her that when my time came I'd be buried beside her. She demanded that right after her funeral I should sleep with another woman and think of her, Gina, at the same time. She made me swear solemnly that I would say Kaddish over her and light a memorial candle. I knew full well that these words roused her sexually. Her flesh turned hot, and she grew fiercely exultant. She cuddled up to me, kissed me, fondled me, and said: "I want to lie in the ground and rot while you, little colt, enjoy yourself! That is my will, my goal. I'll rest easier knowing that you're lying in the arms of women, but one thing I beg of you: Don't forget me. What my grandmother does for me I will do for you—guide and protect you. I'll provide you females with blazing souls and burning bodies. I'll cast them into your net like wiggling fish for you to do with them as your heart desires, but with one proviso—that you don't get married. Why get married? Why tie yourself down? A bee must flit from flower to flower gathering nectar from each. Why should a bee be bound up with one flower? To me you can be bound because I won't be around for long. I don't want you to marry me either. Our souls will remain united forever anyhow. Your pleasure will be my pleasure. . . ."

We barely eked out an existence. I couldn't even afford a laundress, and Gina washed my underwear. She herself wore the old-fashioned clothes because she couldn't afford new dresses. Her apartment hadn't been painted in years and the furniture was broken, but what did this matter to us? At that time there were stores in Warsaw where you could get fantastic bargains. On Old and New Wolowa you could buy a pair of shoes or even a coat (secondhand) for groschens. There were markets where one could get black army bread for half price. Peasant women brought cheese, mushrooms, groats, and onions from the country that one could buy for next to nothing. Gina and I both enjoyed walking. We could walk for miles without getting tired. Riding the trolley was for us a luxury. We rode "Trolley Number 11," which is to say, we walked. We talked about whatever popped into our minds. Gina always headed for the cemetery—either the Jewish one near us or the Catholic one in Powazek; but best of all she liked the Russian Orthodox cemetery far down Leszno Street beyond Karcelak Place. Few Russians remained in Warsaw after Poland gained her independence apart from the Russian refugees, the impoverished "used-to-bes" who were nearly all drunks and slept at the "Circus," an institution for the gentile homeless. Former colonels, generals, and country squires wallowed in the gutters. Gentiles weren't used to living in exile. When a gentile lost his homeland, he became broken spiritually and physically.

But the old Russian cemetery was fenced in, had expensive tombstones and old and thickly branched trees, and represented a symbol of the former Russian might. For some reason the Russians affixed photographs of the deceased to their tombstones. No one came here on the long summer days besides the birds. Gina didn't tire of looking at the tombstones, reading the dates, studying the yellowed photographs. People had died young in the nineteenth century, and many young men and women struck down in their prime were buried here. Nearly all the women wore blouses with high collars, lace, and tall pompadours. A glow of health emanated from their faces and the lust for life characteristic of a ruling race. But they had been cut down in their forties, their thirties, some even in their twenties. Gina stopped before every tombstone and probed, reflected, reckoned. Flecks of sun shone down on her face from between the tree branches. After a while I, too, began to take an interest in the deceased. What had they died from? Had an ongoing epidemic reigned in Warsaw in those days? Had they committed suicide? Or had they died out of longing for Russia? The photographs had faded over the years, but the eyes had retained their animation. They smiled at some secret known only to themselves. It was hard to believe that these young ladies—each of whom knew sections of Pushkin or Lermontov by heart and whose faces expressed such an eagerness for life—were now nothing more than crumbled skeletons, dust. I became temporarily infatuated with these women and contemplated the pleasures they might have provided a man.

Gina pointed to a photograph and said: "Isn't she lovely? Pretty as a picture! Twenty-seven years is all she lived! A lieutenant's wife. What did she die of, eh? He probably betrayed her with every soldier's whore until she wasted away from jealousy. Or maybe he drank the nights away, and her blood became consumed by passion. Look at her, peaches and cream. You can see her firm breasts right through the blouse. You wouldn't poison yourself on her, God forbid, if you lived in those times. Where is she now, eh? Can there be such a thing as a Russian paradise? What would Russians do in paradise?"

"There's no such thing as paradise."

"So you're a heretic again, eh? Just yesterday you said that there is no death. Life is everywhere, even in a stone in the street."

"Yes, true, but she is not in paradise."

"Where, then, in Gehenna?"

"In you, in me, a part of all the stars and planets."

"Words, my dear, mere words. Life is memory. If she doesn't remember that she was Andrej Popov's wife and that Grisha Ivanov inscribed love verses in her album and that she danced at a party with Boris Nikolaevich Saratov, then she is dead. The fact that flowers grow on her mound of earth doesn't make her immortal."

"What would be so good if her soul remembered all the wrongs the lieutenant did her?"

"Don't twist my words! If my grandmother lives, all the grandmothers, grandfathers, and great-grandfathers going back to Adam and even before live, too. They remember everything, but they're so happy up in heaven they forgive all injustices. You yourself said that the souls in the other world love each other and bustle about. Those are your very words."

"That's what the cabala says."

"It's true. You'll see it all with your own eyes. I'll come to you from the other world and give myself to you. I'll be with others, too, with all the men I've ever loved. Your religion of protest begins to displease me. I can accept the craziest notions, but not that God is a malefactor. This doesn't make sense. He sends us down here to suffer a bit, then He rewards us many millions of times over. There are such pleasures awaiting us there that even fantasy cannot describe them. That time when I had the operation and later when I lay sick with the typhus I paid a visit up there above, and I heard such singing that no opera or symphony could compare to it. Angels sang and each note answered all the questions and filled me with a joy no words can convey. I yearned to stay there, but three patriarchs considered

my case and judged that I go back to earth. Their faces emitted a kind of glow that simply doesn't exist here. I began to cry before them, and they consoled and kissed me."

"In your sleep, eh?"

"Awake, awake! There is no such thing as sleep. You don't sleep—you make believe you're sleeping. You don't die, but make believe you're dying. It's all pretense. Just as I suffer and curse my lot, so do I know that it's all nothing on top of nothing. What is suffering? Who is suffering? It's all a kind of game."

"God has no right to make up such games."

"Well, all right, when you stand before Him you'll tell Him so. Come, little colt, I'm hungry. I have some dried noodles and an onion at home, and there should be a bit of cocoa butter left. I'll brown the onion and we'll eat."

"You mean we'll pretend to eat just like the angels at Abraham's."

"Yes, we'll pretend and later we'll pretend we're tired and go to bed and pretend we're terribly in love. What do you say to this philosophy?"

"There is such a philosophy already. Its founder is a man named Vaihinger."

"Who is this Vaihinger? Everything exists already. Give me your mouth. . . ."

13

The government apparently kept an eye on me, for suddenly I received a notice to report for conscription. I knew precisely what this meant—spending two or three years among peasants, all kinds of toughs and wild characters, with no time for reading or writing, and each day putting up with countless insults—all that so a few years later I could give my life for the fatherland. But did a Jew have a fatherland? Some ten or eleven years earlier, my brother Joshua had received a similar demand to sacrifice his life for the Russian fatherland. In the interim Poland had become a part of Germany, and he was nearly drafted to serve the German fatherland. I must be frank here and say that even if Poland were a Jewish nation, I wouldn't have had the slightest urge to be a soldier. For me, a barrack represented a much harsher punishment than prison. Running, jumping, marching, and shooting would be for me an unbearable torture and even worse would be to have to be among people. Just as others constantly required company, so did I require privacy. My whole world concept demanded isolation, the right and the privilege to stay away from others, and time to pursue my probings and nurture my creative appetites. From reading the leftist newspapers and from listening to the communists and their fellow travelers at the Writers' Club I knew that leftism wanted to completely abolish privacy and to institute a perpetual public domain. They constantly spoke of the masses, but my nature demanded the freedom to be alone as long and as often as I wished. Going to heder day after day was to me a burden, nor could I stand the Yeshivas. I doubt that I could have lasted long at a university. At times I envied the peasant with his little plot of ground. I could have been a tailor or shoemaker working in his own shop, but I couldn't for the life of me work in a factory. It's significant to add that despite my strong urge for love and sex, I had remained pathologically bashful.

I resolved that if forced to serve, I would commit suicide first. In the interim I did what many other Jewish recruits had done before me during the Russian occupation—starved myself in order to lose weight and grow weak. I constantly wrangled with Gina. She brought me food even as I was trying to fast. I assumed that the fasting would weaken me sexually, but my libido (a new word that the Freudians had introduced into the daily language) grew stronger instead of weaker. I discovered at that time that the sexual urge is thoroughly bound up with spiritual strength rather than with physical. Love and sex were functions of the soul. The nights were filled with wild fantasies and with an inspiration that negated my pessimistic view of the world. Gina told me that sexual intercourse and particularly the climax evoked visions within her, and I never tired of questioning her about these visions.

She responded: "I see faces, strange countenances."

As loquacious as she was regarding all other matters, she became taciturn when it came to these matters. But why? Did these visions frighten her? Did she lack the words to describe them? As for me, the fasts left me in such a state that the division between sleep and wakefulness just about disappeared. The moment I closed my eyes I promptly began to dream. I saw giants with heads reaching to the clouds. They wore clothes not of our time and perhaps not even of this world. They marched along in what seemed a kind of cosmic funeral procession and grunted a dirge rife with melancholy. Sometimes I saw swarms of dwarfs who sang, danced, and rejoiced in an unearthly rapture. These visions were so real, so magnificent, so richly detailed. True, they quickly faded from memory, but they left me perplexed and with the feeling that sleep erases all limitations of time, space, and causality. At times I dreamed of slaughters, massacres, pogroms, and awoke trembling, yet charged with renewed lust. Gina awoke at precisely the same split second, and we fell upon one another with a hunger that astounded us. What a remarkable mechanism was the brain! How extravagant it became the moment one closed his eyes! I often resolved to write down my dreams, yet at the same time I knew

that this would be impossible. The moment I opened my eyes they burst like soap bubbles, immediately dissolved, and vanished. Nor did the words exist in my vocabulary to paint a true picture of a dream.

Most philosophers spoke with contempt of human emotion; others ignored it altogether. Our holy books maintained that evil thoughts emanated from the evil spirit. The *Literary Pages* printed constant articles about Freud, who had begun to take dreams and emotions seriously, but his approach was rationalistic. He tried to analyze something that couldn't be grasped, that lacked substance. He tried to make generalizations in an area thoroughly individualistic, one of unique occurrence, and infinitely ambiguous. That which the cabalists attributed to God applied to a dream as well—no words could be found to describe it. The best you could do was to keep silent about it.

Spring turned into summer and the heat waves commenced in Warsaw. The days stretched endlessly, the twilight lingered seemingly forever, and the sky stayed light until 10 P.M. I ate a spare supper. Gina played awhile with her table and tried to write automatically. I stood at the open window staring down at Gesia Street. The funerals kept on all day. Not far from here rested the old corpses and the new, among them Reb Dov Ber Meisels, my great-great-grandfather and the Warsaw rabbi. Balmy breezes wafted up to my nostrils, and I kept thinking that they bore the stench of rot and decay, along with the secrets of birth and death. The street was dark and stars twinkled over the tin rooftops. At times it seemed to me that I could make out the white sash called the Milky Way. Everything was near—death, the universe, the enigma of dreams, the illusion of love and sex. Dogs barked, cats meowed. Gina's apartment swarmed with moths, gnats, and beetles. Insects flew in through the open windows to make a final flutter before dying. Gina and I both sought to unite with the forces that guided the earth and to come to some kind of accounting and conclusions regarding the world, but these forces would have none of it. We were condemned to remain sunk forever in chaos.

Although Gina didn't conduct herself according to the laws of the Shulchan Aruch, she still mumbled her nightly prayers. I mentally begged God to save me from the barracks and at the same time prayed for those forced to stay there. So many dangers and problems lurked for everyone! A moment didn't go by without some kind of trouble. People themselves caused one another grief. All the jails were jammed with criminals. At times I heard gunfire in the night, screams and blows, cries for help. The communists in Warsaw sought every means of fomenting a revolution and turning Poland over to the Bolsheviks. Hitler and his Nazis had already formulated plans to take back Upper Silesia and the "corridor" that the Versailles Treaty had stripped from Germany. Polish anti-Semites agitated against the Jews. The Jewish political parties wrangled among themselves. The Lithuanians yearned to seize Vilno. The Ruthenians and White Russians waged a struggle against Polish rule. Hobbes was right—everyone waged war against everyone else. Every peace was rife with new wars. The leaders themselves were at each other's throats. I couldn't live in this world—merely smuggle myself through life slithering like gnats and mice, actually like all the creatures. Each day I got through was—and has remained to this day—a miracle. Jewish history in particular was one mighty travail of smuggling and sneaking through nations and laws that condemned us to death. Before going to sleep I took a last look at the starry sky. Was it this way up there, too? Was there an island of peace somewhere in the universe? . . .

I went to bed, but Gina went on bustling a good deal longer. She washed the dishes, darned and washed her and my underwear. I lay there in the dark with my ears cocked. Maybe God would speak to me. Maybe my great-great-grandfather in the cemetery would tell me something. Maybe I would come up with something like a second Newtonian formula which would unravel the mystery of the world. This revelation was likely to be much simpler than one might imagine. It might consist of one sentence. I even had a notion in what direction the formula would go—there was no death. The "I" was a thoroughgoing illusion. Sufferings were pleasures. Today, yesterday, and tomorrow were one and the same. I, Rothschild, the mouse in its hole, the bedbug on the wall, and the corpse in the grave were identical in every sense, as were dream and reality, male and female, thoughts and stones, feelings and atoms, love and hate. Well, but it wasn't enough to say this—it had to be proven. Leibnitz couldn't do it. Spinoza's geometric method wasn't convincing. This formula had to be written not in words and numbers but in some other medium that I would first have to invent. It was altogether possible that it had already been invented on some distant planet. . . .

I began to doze off, and the formula came to me in a dream: that which we called death was life, and that which we called life was death. The stone in the street lived and I was a corpse. The stone didn't hope nor suffer; for it, time, space, and casuality didn't exist. It didn't have to eat; it needed no apartment; it was part of the mighty, extensive life that was the universe. That which we called life was a scab, an itching, a poisonous toadstool that grew on old planets. The earth suffered from an eczema of its skin. From time to time it scratched itself causing an earthquake or a flood, but there was no danger of this eczema penetrating deeper or of infecting other planets. The prognosis was a favorable one. All that was required was that for a few minutes the earth should grow a few hundred degrees hotter or colder on its outer surface. The earth could easily manage this, but the eczema was so light and the earth so involved with its activities that she neglected to do this

since the eczema might one day vanish of its own. The symptoms of this eczema were quite familiar to the cosmic medicine—a little dust on the surface became ill and transformed into consciousness, which in God's dictionary was a synonym for death, protest, goals, suffering, doubting, asking countless questions and growing entangled in endless contradictions. . . .

I had fallen asleep and Gina woke me. She had washed up in the kitchen and her flesh felt damp and cool. We embraced and lay silent for a long time, then Gina said: "Little colt, I made a decision today that may change my whole life and maybe yours, too."

"What kind of decision?" I asked, and she said: "I want to have a child with you. . . ."